February 17, 2005

Dear Patricia and Donald,

The rich and powerful have stolen the BEST from God's Term, and replaced the BEST with god-Silver and traditional dogma.

"I say it again, it is easier for a camel to go through the eye of a needle than for a rich man to enter the Kingdom of God!" This remark confounded the disciples. MATTHEW 19:25

The disciples were Confused! How much more are we.

Bless you in your journey to understanding.

Pat

February 7, 2005

ZECHARIAH 5:1-4

by

PAT HOCKEL

authorHOUSE™

1663 LIBERTY DRIVE, SUITE 200
BLOOMINGTON, INDIANA 47403
(800) 839-8640
WWW.AUTHORHOUSE.COM

This book is a work of non-fiction. Names of people and places have been changed to protect their privacy.

© 2004 PAT HOCKEL
All Rights Reserved.

No part of this book may be reproduced, stored in a retrieval system, or transmitted by any means without the written permission of the author.

First published by AuthorHouse 11/10/04

ISBN: 1-4184-6626-3 (e)
ISBN: 1-4184-3086-2 (sc)
ISBN: 1-4184-3087-0 (dj)

Library of Congress Control Number: 2004105061

Printed in the United States of America
Bloomington, Indiana

This book is printed on acid-free paper.

Acknowledgements

Thank you psychologist, Harlen Brenden, for posing the challenge before me to "trust myself." Do you remember how stunned I was at such a thought? I pray your seed, Dr. Brenden, landed on fertile ground.

I cannot fully express my gratitude to you, Scottie Anderson. Tirelessly, without a complaint, you transformed my journaling English into proper English. Thank you for undoing thirty years of undisciplined punctuation.

Thank you, Tyndale House Publishers and all who contributed to The Book, a special edition of The Living Bible. Without the interpretation communicated on those pages I doubt if "God's Word" would have left such a life altering impact on me.

And more "thanks" than words can express to my parents, who are not here to love anymore, and two daughters. My parents allowed me the freedom to travel into the future with the knowledge that their LOVE was unconditional. My dear daughters have been the joy in my life and a reason to contemplate the beauty of tomorrow. Their continuous struggle to do GOOD, brings tears of joy to my eyes. Press on, dear ones.

And, Thank You, Peter, for all of the "firsts" and teaching me about things I never would have fathomed do exist, are "real" and are a part of "The Kingdom of God."

Table Of Contents

ACKNOWLEDGEMENTS		v
INTRODUCTION		ix
I	HUMANS MAKE MISTAKES, CENTURIES OF MISTAKES	1
II	YOU RAISE ME UP TO WALK ON STORMY SEAS	19
III	LOVE KNOWS	35
IV	THIS IS THE AIR I BREATHE	51
V	GOD'S WAY IS TRUTH, TRUTH IS GOD'S WAY	71
VI	READY LORD, I'M READY LORD TO FOLLOW WHERE YOU LEAD	83
VII	WILL I SING HALLELUJAH? WILL I BE ABLE TO SPEAK AT ALL?	99
VIII	WE HAVE BEEN TOLD, WE'VE SEEN HIS FACE	109
IX	ON EAGLE'S WINGS	121
X	GOD IS THE LIGHT WHEN DAY TURNS TO NIGHT	143
EPILOGUE		155
Post Script:		157

INTRODUCTION

I can't remember when I accepted that absolutely every step we take in our lives, prepares us for what God has in store for us in the future; every joy, every pain, every fear, leaves its mark for future reference. I was about eight years old when I watched the movie about Peter Marshall, the head chaplain in Congress in 1948, until his death in 1949, and how his faith in God led him and his wife through their trials in life. Having lived, by this tender age, in the pain of my parents lives, witnessing the destructive sibling relationships of my mother, feeling the futility of trying to please people that don't really want to be "pleased," and seeing first hand, the effects of shattered dreams (my younger sister was unable to respond to the world secondary to brain damage from hydrocephalus), Peter and his wife gave me a goal in life; I had to know God, INTIMATELY.

The people in my formative years believed they knew and were pleasing to God, yet, even though their generation had been born in the United States where "freedom" to follow God the way they believed was right, was one of the reasons for being here, were still suffering from the discrimination of one religion marrying the wrong religion, wounds that hadn't healed in the forty years following the disgrace of "having to get married," the rage of being the "un-favorite-child," and the destruction of never acknowledging reality ("if you can't say something good, don't say anything at all"). I knew when, and if, I found God, God wasn't going to be the same God they thought they knew. Something was very wrong, so very, very wrong, in what they believed was right. I promised God, and myself where're God was, that I would keep an open mind and listen to everything around and in me to lead the way. When I made that promise, I had NO clue that I would make devastating choices in my early adulthood because of the lack of a third necessary ingredient – TRUST. I had to learn to trust what my mind heard and saw, trust God was leading the way, enough to make choices accordingly. Thanks to Dr. Brendon,, I was able to add trust and act to my commitment of look and listen.

What has transpired in my life because of this commitment is, all at the same time, terrifying, exhilarating, painful, ecstatic, tragic, gloriously awesome, joyful, sad, energizing, exhausting, and would be completely overwhelming if it weren't for G O D, J E S U S, and the H O L Y S P I R I T . (I really have needed all three! plus a few Angels thrown in here and there! and once, so I'm told, an army of Angels!) The end of my story won't be until the day I leave this earth, but just in case what God has told me "will happen," does happen, God (and me, too) want YOU to have the history of the serendipitous circumstances that brought me to this degree of "Trust-in-God" so YOU can have a better chance of **recognizing** your path to God, recognizing GOD. For I need to "Praise God" continuously (to you and myself) for how happy God has made me! Yes indeed, despite my lack of confidence, God has clothed me with garments of salvation and draped about me the robe of righteousness, even though, most often, what I am feeling is a sense of trembling awe at being given the privilege of walking humbly with Thee.

Isaiah 61:10

I
HUMANS MAKE MISTAKES, CENTURIES OF MISTAKES

It will be no secret by the end of these writings that the purpose of these memoirs is to announce, concisely, that God, our Lord and Savior Jesus Christ, and the Holy Spirit are angry with the leaders, priests, assayers of information, and loyal supporters there of, of one of His Temples, the Roman Catholic Church.

God's people, if they could give *credibility* to what they see and hear and if they would search for *truth* instead of following the lead of those whose worldly future depends on the power and status of the Roman Catholic Church, should have this message just by listening to the five and ten p.m. news and watching the Financial Reports published each week in their Catholic Church bulletins. Although *now*, the leaders of our Temple are hiding behind the War on Terrorism and Iraq, Statute of Limitation laws, the complaining economy, tainted statistics, a polished Catholic press, and they are side tracking the media with their return to aggressively throttling Catholics with legalistic maneuvers (who can receive communion in the Roman Catholic Church?). Their strategies for avoiding media attention are so good; it feels like we have already forgotten the horrendously shocking results of the John Jay report (an independent audit of the records of every diocese in the United States for evidence of reported cases of priest/child molestation and the hierarchies response to those reports)!

When I actively went searching for "*What does God want?*" it was to find answers for personal pains, NOT to run head-on into Catholic Church tradition and the ramifications of their traditions. Evidently the pain and resulting growth have something God wants me to share, for only recently has the realization from God's messages blatantly pointed out that as many as are willing to understand *where* God is found, need to have the opportunity to know where to look. The reason is obvious, of course; God loves His children and wants as many to come home to Him as will or can come.

My motivations for finding God were not so pure as to be concerned about the whole human race; my motivations were self-centered, albeit genuine; they were desperate, albeit with much patience to go where God led; my motivations were to neutralize the fear of the unknown and future, albeit, *trusting* God. And most important, my motivation was to understand where God fit into the powerful *state of being*, what the world has minimized to F A L L I N G I N   L O V E, Physical Attraction, Good Chemistry, EROS or Limerance.[1] Whatever the world names it, I found myself *there*, with no way out, no way in and no way.

What I have discovered in life experience about this "falling in love" parallels the discovery last year, 2003, of what was believed for the last thirty to forty years about Hormone Replacement Therapy during menopause, very beneficial, is the exact opposite; it frequently triggers breast cancer and heart disease. Doctors would actually groan if a woman chose to go the natural route through menopause and not take hormones. What I believed about romantic love the first thirty plus years of my life is what was taught by professionals, psychological and religious, only to discover they were wrong, dead wrong; and what they did describe was

---

[1] A name given this condition by Dorothy Tennov in her book describing her discernments of the results of her years of study of the condition. The book is entitled Love and Limerence, copyright 1979.

bland and very incomplete compared to the real thing. Being those I (and most of society) trusted were so wrong about the more obvious elements, what other misconceptions were/are they promoting as reality? What were/are they basing their educated opinions on? Why were their studies giving such erroneous information? Why were/are they working so hard to believe what they state are their beliefs? My mind couldn't and can't stop asking questions.

I'm sure most of you have read the poem, <u>Footprints In The Sand.</u> For the last twenty plus years of my life there has only been one set of footprints; I have not had the physical or emotional strength to take one step on my own. The advice of the world (psychologists, friends, self-help books and books and books, relatives, church teachings) did not prove entirely true.

What I was told by the world:	**What was/is manifested in life:**
TIME HEALS	Not while the one you are ONE with is alive, anyway. It's more like I just adapted to living with pain and those around me believe it is gone. It's very similar to living with severe arthritis. The people you are living with don't see or understand the debilitating pain, or the tremendous amount of energy the pain consumes, if one is going to keep moving. At least when arthritis exists, one has something tangible to blame the decreased productivity on.
IT'S just physical attraction (pheromones, attraction to the others physical make-up and mannerisms, addiction to the dopamine those attractions produce in the body)	That doesn't explain non-verbal instant messaging, or serendipitous happenings. It also contradicts falling in love with a paraplegic, burn victim with massive skin distortions, etc., all of which, has and does happen.

THE FLYING SCROLL

"Falling in love" happens over and over again. Its average life span is about seven years.

In whose book? I had mistaken *pseudo*-in love (*psuedo*-in love will be defined on the following pages), in my past, for the REAL THING, so I presume many have. Real Love makes pseudo-*in love* look like a Tinker Toy. The pseudo-*in love* did last about seven years. When Real Love happens, there is NO DOUBT what it is; the symptoms, as a package, do not exist in any other realm of life and a soul does not tire of another soul. Physical maiming, disease, poverty, conflicting beliefs, color of skin, etc., have no effect on the HEALING power of contact with each other. New revelations may surface before I die, but after twenty plus years of this condition, with the lessons learned during those years, I seriously doubt it.

'in love' is BLIND

Actually, I found the opposite to be true. "Blindness" is an erroneous term used to describe how relentless the spirit of a person becomes to give to the other person every opportunity possible to see *goodness* and *what is right* and behave and make decisions accordingly. HOPE lasts a long time!

My real inspirational moments are right when I wake up in the morning. Almost before I'm fully conscious and the activities of daily living consume the rest of my thinking space, solutions to problems pop in, decisions have been made and puzzling situations are often clear. When I found myself in this unwanted condition, *in love,* morning after morning the first thought was, "Good Lord, all these years have I been DEAD WRONG about *love*? Would anyone believe me if I told them what I have been experiencing? I wouldn't believe me if it wasn't me having the experience."

I fought the condition day and night with all I had, but it wasn't enough. I didn't want it. I didn't want to change my life-style to accommodate it. I started wearing a rubber band on my wrist and would snap it over and over again when intrusive thoughts interrupted where I wanted my mind to be. I sought counseling; I prayed; I started reading book after book in hopes I could find some helpful information, in the hope I would become more powerful than the condition. All I found was man's communication tools have no way to communicate IT; man tries in song, literature (some, transferred to the big screen), lyric, poem and love letters, but quite unsuccessfully. The only thing close was God's Word in the Bible.

THE BIBLE?

This discovery un-did me for a long, long period of time. It feels like running a red light we are so conditioned to stop; I still stiffen at the thought of sharing this discovery; I feel I'm going to be broadsided in a fatal collision I caused. But God says, "Do not be afraid, for I am with you always." I pray sharing the anguish of my soul helps you to find our Lord and Savior, too. I mean *REALLY* find God... to carry you through this world. Every religion that believes in a Supreme Power is full of hints on where God is and all of them fall off or are kicked off the cliff of awareness right before our eyes *behold*.

Power doesn't want you to see; *money* doesn't want you to see; *tradition* doesn't want you to see. Aren't *power* and *money* considered *idols*? And didn't Jesus acknowledge one of the reasons He was sent to earth was to eliminate some of the traditional rituals of the Jews? This tells me there is *a lot* in **tradition** reeking of idolatry, also. And if the words on these pages say to you, you have been *dead wrong* about what you believe, like when I woke up with this awareness morning after morning, your reflex response will be to refuse to *see,* too. I pray you can leave a door open to possibility as you read these pages and experience life.

Self-doubt about what I was experiencing became a driving force to find some credible information. The voluminous attempts by mankind to communicate in this arena are astounding, yet nothing I found conveyed near the state of being in which I found myself. Yes, there was elements mentioned that were a part of this *state,* but something HUGE was not being communicated in any circle, religious or not.

In order to expand on these thoughts, the following relationships need to be acknowledged:

Consider the relationship of:

the electron to the atom,

the moon to the earth,

the earth to the sun,

the sun to the center of the Cosmos.

Those relationships helped me know, being God made the atom, the earth, the moon, and the sun, He very likely meant His Word to have a similar relationship to:

the *plane of the individual,*

the *plane of the family,*

the *plane of the community,*

the *plane of the nation,*

the *plane of the world* and

the *plane of the spiritual realm,* which returns, via a circle, back to the *plane of the individual.*

Also, before I expand on the learned concepts further, I need to clarify the following: I share this with reluctance; because, clarifying this piece may prevent some from reading further, which will precipitate the loss of valuable insights. This piece? God is neither male nor female; more accurately, God is both. I need to acknowledge this because of the confines of language. There is no language to expand on God's messages without using our gender-based language. Therefore, in referencing God please understand, when I use "He," "His," or "Him," with capital letters, I really do mean God is complete, is both male and female, God is the great "I AM."

Finding no other source to relieve the pain, I started reading the Bible and applying God's words/messages to each *plane.* The help I was looking for from our Lord gradually came into focus and was right in front of me on the pages of the Bible lying on my lap; it was there where God teaches us about this state in which I find myself. I was and am in awe. When I applied whatever God was saying to each *plane,* new *life giving* light bulbs commenced lighting up and have not stopped.

This concept was actually Jesus' teaching tool; His parables were an explanation of a situation on one *plane* (where the listeners had understanding) and then He paralleled this understood situation to a situation on another *plane* (where the listeners were in confusion), which resulted in understanding. When I realized this at a more conscious level, I started to apply His Words that were on the *plane of the community* to the *plane of the individual* or were on the *plane of the world* to the *plane of the family* and so on. Now God's Word is *never ending,* literally.

So, why has my *love life* so profoundly, with the energy of an atomic bomb, catapulted me into the arena of Roman Catholic Church law? On one end of the spectrum it is, "What does God want?" and on the other end of the spectrum, it is what I am not sure I have accepted yet; my *core* has not accepted, my love for Peter[2] is my love for a Roman Catholic priest. My insides screamed over and over to whomever, whatever might hear, "What do you mean he is a priest, a Roman Catholic priest, nooooooo."

In various visions, intrusive mille-second mental images throughout my young adult life (probably from eighteen years of age till I met him fifteen years later), **his** were the eyes always watching, **his** was the silhouette observing from a distance, **his** profile was of the one telling me I wasn't where I was suppose to be so he had to stay away. The vision, which left its biggest mark on me (this was about nine years before I met Peter), happened during the last days I was carrying my oldest daughter, when I was just about to give birth. I was standing by the curb waiting for my ride when the car parked in front of me started to pull away and paused before entering the street. I had to take a double take as the person driving the car had familiar features, but yet, weren't. The words passing through my mind were as though the driver of this vehicle was saying to me, "I have to go, I can't interfere, there's been a huge mistake!" Whoever this was turned his face away so I couldn't get a good look at his features. I was left in a confusing fog of sadness that hung over me for a long, long time. I didn't understand, but something rang so true I had a very difficult time dismissing the event. You see, neither the car nor driver were *"real,"* so it wasn't a case of mistaken identity. For a number of years the memory of this vision and the sadness it brought would surface, but eventually (it took years), I buried its memory. Thus it was quite a shock when the owner of these eyes, this silhouette, and this profile - belonged to a priest. It still feels like a cosmic joke. When the enlightenment surfaced of this soul in front of me (Peter) being the one in those visions, even then it felt like an un-preventable tragedy.

---

[2] The name chosen for my love because, like the Apostle Peter, even though he loved Jesus Christ, he denied him. Also, Peter Marshall comes to mind. Somewhere inside, he has the equivalent of Peter Marshall, alive and well.

Oh, I doubted the recognition, but everything he did reinforced something in him had made a *soul recognition,* too. From the look on his face of joyful shock when our eyes met the very first time to his hyperventilating when sitting next to me at a church committee meeting, to having his body freeze-in-position with the communion host raised in mid air, because his eye caught mine. During one service, as he lifted the *Body of Christ in Praise,* he experienced something overwhelmingly powerful concerning me; his face distorted, he took a deep breath and held it, and his arms froze in mid air like he feared other parts of him would involuntarily move if he signaled one muscle to direct his arms to descend. After he gained control and safely, smoothly brought his arms down, his eyes met mine and his eyes were filled with a stunned glare. Either he could not believe an emotion/feeling in himself with those characteristics had any value and dismissed it immediately, or he invalidated the experience by reminding himself, this is *the experience* he had vowed to sacrifice. I'll never know, as he never shared his experience with me. There are so many memories; if reliving them were my purpose it wouldn't be difficult to fill a few hundred pages, but it is not. What I would have written on those few hundred pages, though, is what convinced me I had better follow God/Jesus Christ/the Holy Spirit wherever our sovereign power led or this *blessing* was for naught, and my demise was at hand.

Following God? As you well know there isn't a black and white formula to accomplish that. On the *plane of the individual,* other than *Humanae Vitae and, now, Theology of the Body,* there isn't much seeping out of Rome to help. Even those were a response to support "No Birth control" and "Marriage is between a man and a woman" issues, respectively, than how to *follow God* in our individual, intimately personal choices on who we should marry. *Theology of the Body,* it may be argued, addresses the *plane of the individual,* but only after the marriage contract is signed, after the choice has been made and declared *covenant* material by the church and society. What about *before* the choice is made? when there is still a choice to be made? The only official warning I have heard from Rome is on the *plane of the community,* beware of Muslim and non-Christian attachments.

Shouldn't the church be teaching the characteristics of intimate sexual desires to be cognizant of **before** marriage, before the decision, vow, has been made? The church does perpetrate the perspective that if one is true to church law all will turn out for the *best* (fidelity until after marriage, attending Mass every Sunday and Holy Day of Obligation, etc.) The lack of relationship characteristics to heed combined with changing the description of a sacrament for the Sacrament of Marriage, while one is deciding, gives the **non-verbal** message, "The Sacrament of Marriage causes or allows *in love* feelings. *In love* feelings will develop and cause intimate, ONE BODY sexual experiences when you follow our laws." **At some level, I involuntarily heard and unconsciously believed this non-verbal message before I was married, and it is NOT TRUE.** Humanity does need the church to be a primary messenger on how to recognize God's calling to the lifetime mate God wills us to share life with. We need to have a clear view of the signs and symptoms on how to recognize who we allow ourselves to marry, for if total, whole being, intimate feelings and desires weren't present before marriage, they surely won't be present after marriage. But before the church can be our teacher and guide, the church needs to accept the importance of the *whole being in love.*

Yes, this feels like and many times is dangerous territory. Since the human race is presently in a state of naiveté ness with no language to help and no help available, *before one has experienced* the *whole,* there is an **almost indescribable** difference between simple physical sexual desires combined with friendship and the total, whole being, intimate, emotionally connected, and *referencing God* needs to be in the equation to describe, sexual desires. After one has experienced the *whole,* there is no doubt and there never will be again, of *what is what.* When one is young and new to sexuality, just the thought of the word "sex" triggers the body; causing much confusion about what is what. When one adds, participating in sexual intercourse silently alters a person immensely, and the person with whom you shared intercourse is not a natural part of your life (spouse), it's like giving a chunk of your soul away with nothing to fill the hole where the *chunk* used to be. In trying to know what feeling(s) to give credibility to, this causes more confusion. *Knowledge* can alter this element. In many to most cases in a mentally healthy, <u>mature</u> person (30-40 years old), the *whole being in-love* is a necessary ingredient for the body, especially the body of a woman, to be a fully participating partner in sexual intimacy. Secondary to the frequent television adds about Viagra, Cialas and Levitra, it feels safe to surmise, *the whole being in-love* is needed by mature men, also. The conscious mind may try to deceive the body, but more than we acknowledge the body obeys the subconscious, so will not allow it. (Between antidepressants and sexual stimulators, the drug companies have made a *killing*! There is NO WAY drug companies want the importance of *the whole being "in love", God is in the equation "in love"* union to leak out to the general public! They would lose billions of dollars.) As with my own experience, when the experience is the teacher of truth, there are unpleasant, if not tragic, consequences. On the *plane of the individual,* religions (many originated in Catholicism), to maintain and increase their following and maintain their power over an individual's mind, have perpetrated this intimate, private, next to the soul place (total, whole being intimate sexuality) does not exist (it is a figment of the imagination) or it and its desires are evil. Catholicism does not talk about it; Catholicism does not reference any *good* from it in any ones life; Catholicism actually mocks the *whole,* if with nothing else, with their silence.

If intentions are pure, why have I NEVER heard a homily praising the <u>Song of Solomon</u> in the *plane of the individual* where it is written? What makes this an important question is, the material for teaching the value of *whole being in-love* eroticism is available at the church's ROOTS, the Bible! The hierarchy validates all their other choices by referencing the content of the Bible, yet they have gone out of their way to invalidate what doesn't even need a keen mind to understand, the core message as it is written in the Song of Solomon. Why?

The first time I even knew this book existed was when I decided to read the Bible in the privacy of my own home. What is so threatening in its content that no one, especially clergy, dares to dissect it? When someone does dare to reference it, the clergy's response is, always, it is (only) an allegory of God's love for His church; why not *love* between a man and woman and God's love for His church? Wouldn't it be a revelation that it's GOD IN BOTH? In reality, giving both total credibility elevates *whole being in-love* to never before seen heights (on the ladder of importance) to discern God's will. The Song of Solomon is even written in the *plane of the individual,* so it can be surmised that this *plane* needs to be first priority, before applying its allegory messages to *the plane of the community. This is HUGE!* Being this book so beautifully references such a core part of each of us, isn't it logical to believe it was inspired by God to tune us into a sacred part of us? And tell us, "Yes, this is from me, the essence of me in you."

When God is IN the equation comprising *erotic love,*[3] I need to give it a new name; for this book I will name it **_Life Light Love (LLL)._**

Why hasn't the Roman Catholic Church and society put more value on The Song of Solomon? More accurately, why has religion, especially the Roman Catholic Church, **erased** the value of The Song of Solomon? Here are some probabilities:

    1.)   The *rich and powerful are* who finance the church. The *rich and powerful* refuse to give any power to **Life Light Love** for God may not plan a mate for their son or daughter they would want. The *rich and powerful* demand their offspring

---

[3] The name used to reference romantic love by C.S. Lewis in his book The Four Loves.

marry the *rich and powerful* and would not give any money to an institution, who told them they had to honor God's will if God's will went against their earthly goals for their off spring. If it weren't for science discovering the cause of hemophilia, the world's royalty would still marry their relatives to insure their wealth and power stayed where they wanted it - in their families. The money the Roman Catholic Church makes because its clergy is celibate is a pebble on the floor of a huge gravel truck, in comparison to the money given to the church to instill in the off spring that **LLL** is to be disregarded or minimized as much as possible in making marriage decisions. Of course, the rhetoric of those who want control includes the word *love*, but with the boundaries they put on it (same religion, same affluence and status, same interests, etc. and **NO** instruction on how to recognize **LLL**), they manipulatively exclude **LLL**.

2.) A huge majority of the world's parents have been, and many remain adamant their children marry within their race, and do not want any overt evidence an inter-racial marriage should be supported because God wills it, **LLL**.

3.) How many of you, who are from a Catholic family, saw your parent's eyes light up when you announced you were dating someone who was Catholic? (Children WANT to please their parents!) How many of you were told you should only date someone who is Catholic? It is *nye* impossible for a Catholic parent to say, "Bless you for pleasing God by marrying this Lutheran because you two have a God inspired union." "Thank you God! for blurring religious boundaries." But the adults now affecting our young came from the time when these boundaries were much stronger.

4.) Throughout history, those in control want as many children born into their society as possible. The larger the harvest of children, the more soldiers available to fight for and protect their riches. These leaders want as many to agree to marriage and family as possible, therefore the leaders cannot promote LLL as the queue for marriage for there wouldn't be as many marriages and those who did marry would, more than likely, marry at an older age, allowing fewer children to be born to each union. This would result in a drastic decrease in the birthrate. In history, kings would have abolished Catholicism if they supported a belief, which resulted in a diminished birthrate. (This strategy, negating the validity of LLL as criteria for marriage, did not miss the minds of the princes of the Roman Catholic Church – for it works!) A populace too large for a countries economy is healthy for that countries armies; a hungry young man is a welcome sight to an army's recruiter.

5.) Diminished birthrate would allow each child more opportunity to excel in this world; LLL marriages would give male and female relationships a happier, more joyful image. This combination would result in even fewer souls willing to fight in an army, as well as, commit to unconditional celibacy. The happier the people are in the existing society, the fewer volunteers willing to sacrifice their lives to any religion. The church definitely advantages from a discontented, *in pain*, hurting society.

6.) A testimony to the last two perspectives, perpetrating the erroneous belief that God wants non-LLL marriage unions (which guarantees more marriages to increase population, thus giving any religion more power) is one of the most evil people in the history of mankind, Hitler. He latched onto Catholicism's promotion of no birth control and large families. He rewarded woman for each child they birthed with a prestigious emblem to wear on their outerwear, the more children, the more prestigious the emblem. Hitler understood the power of numbers and so does the Roman Catholic Church; in fact, Hitler learned this from the Roman Catholic Church. As mentioned in number five, when LLL is the criteria for marriage, most likely, people will not marry early enough in life to have a large number of children – a condition those in control of the masses, who need solders or vowed priests, do NOT want. The powers of the world have greatly benefited from society, especially the young, being confused about sexuality and "*in love.*"

On the *plane of the community*, as much as our cultures have tried to destroy *in-love* relationships, viewing its affects from God's vantage point we actually owe LLL *"past due mega"* thanks. IT is probably the only *caring* reason why any culture has initiated peaceful communication with another culture throughout history. Not only have the two that found LLL (or should I say LLL found them?), crossed boundaries to be together, the children of these dual (culture, race, monetary roots, religion, etc.,) marriages are people who are more likely to have a deep understanding and appreciation for *both sides* of the different, conflicting life styles and know to their core, all humans are more alike than different. From the generational perspective, LLL is breaking down the boundaries of the world, the off-spring of those crossing boundaries to marry are taking the best from each of their source worlds to apply to life now and in the future. Doesn't this cosmic-like plan sound like something only God would instigate?

Now? God has me praying for the lawmakers in His Temples. I am to pray they change their laws to be compatible to God's will as individually manifested in each one of God's children. Yes, I am to pray the lawmakers in the Roman Catholic Church change the law forcing priests and nuns to live a celibate life style. For when the blessing of **LLL** is the road God gives to someone to experience God's Light and Love and accomplish His will, Catholicism has erased the road. Not immediately, maybe even a generation or more later, painful to God, sinful *states of being* surface (*pedophiles, homosexuality, incest, womanizers,* etc.) from the way those, who lost their way (because the road had been erased), dealt with the resulting pain; God has had enough! Even though He loves His Temple, God has called *Judgment* (lawsuits, damaged image and straining chauffeurs are only the beginning) on it; God is mandating *no more innocent victims.*

Punishing the church this severely was not an overnight, spontaneous action. Our merciful God does give warnings; one huge warning was/is the AIDS epidemic. I am a registered nurse in a 250 bed hospital and in the early to mid eighties the nine patients I had direct contact with, during the first three to five years HIV was claiming lives in the Minneapolis and St. Paul metro area, had contracted the disease through homosexual relationships and were either raised or presently active in the Roman Catholic Church. That's 100% of my contact with HIV positive patients in a Protestant hospital, in a Protestant community. During this time I was on the Intravenous Therapy Team and had contact with all the patients who had IV's in the entire hospital, which were all the HIV positive patients. During these years, the choir director at the parish I was attending also died from AIDS. The inner circle of the church, the choir members, committee members, etc., knew he was homosexual, but believed him when he said he was suffering from cancer. Not until the terminal stage did he announce it was AIDS claiming his life. Over the years I have been watchful for any statistical information as to whether any group of people has a higher percentage of those suffering or deceased from HIV than others. Other than an article from Texas referencing an increased percentage in Catholic priests, I have not seen any other groups mentioned. Could it be, my observation of the number of afflicted being a drastically high percentage of Catholics be an isolated situation? I don't think so! Yes, there were isolated non-Catholic cases I had heard about, outside of work, over the years, but the percentage of the ones being Catholic throughout the world should have given a warning to Rome that *something catastrophic is wrong.* If history applies *now*, as it usually does, and from the evidence revealed at the Bishops Conference in Texas in 2002, combined with Rome promoting Cardinal Law and giving him an increase in annual income, the evidence supports the hierarchy does NOT want to change **anything** so they continue to put blindfolds on and claim ignorance. God must have been totally dismayed when the ingrained official culture of the Roman Catholic Church even ignored the AIDS epidemic to protect their image and their life style. How can they ignore their perspective on sexuality is causing sexual dysfunction, which is living in a constant state of pain, in too many of its members to be coincidence; how can their **image** be that paramount? Pope John Paul II states he doesn't believe in accidents. So why doesn't he apply his philosophy to the sexual sickness in the church and take steps to discover the cause. He is smart enough to know it is NOT only an issue of discipline. He has to be smart enough to know the magnitude of the present crisis is *bigger* than **discipline**. I ponder what he is protecting.

II
YOU RAISE ME UP TO WALK ON STORMY SEAS

"The celibacy restrictions are not up for discussion." With these words of Pope John Paul II in my mind, I watch these princes of the church and my mind can hear their rationalizations about the celibate choices they have made. They are as human as we are so, for most of them, there had to be doors they closed in their lives, vault doors they slammed shut and locked, which otherwise would have led to a significant other, a marriage spouse, to share life experiences. For example, I can see them saying to themselves as they reflect on the value of their choices, "Mary, the one he had experienced LLL with, married another and had twelve children and apparently is happy. Therefore, God really did want me to follow this celibate path." This prince doesn't see any connection between Mary's gay son and her workaholic husband with his decision to abandon Mary.[4] The prince, and this could be any priest, spends *a lot* of energy to only see she is *fine* without him; he spends *a lot* of energy to believe "It was meant to be the way it is, God is pleased," so he doesn't feel guilty about his choices.

---

[4] See the reference to John Bradshaw's teachings about one of the causes of homosexuality in Chapter V, God's Way Is Truth, Truth Is God's Way, pages 73-74.

Another possibility? Maybe *Mary* joined the convent after the vowed cleric's, the prince's departure. Wow! This prince feels he has done double duty for God and the church. This *Mary* was at least hearing God well enough to know she wouldn't be able to give her **all** to another man, anyway. Or like a nun serving a parish I was part of, she wasn't going to allow herself to go through *pain* like that again so she placed herself in, what she believed, was *safe territory* to avoid any possibility. What is nauseating about this scenario is the pride the prince feels about **his** choice. He refuses to see this world should have been a place where he and Mary could have accomplished good for God, together. He refuses to see what would have transpired if he had made the choice to follow God's **will** to be in Mary's life and vise-versa. His absence from the priesthood may have contributed to the church laws allowing married clergy decades, maybe centuries, earlier than is happening. Then he could see the pain he would have saved the children of God in this present day. What is lost **forever** is **what** their combined energy would have produced for God on the *plane of the community,* and for them, on the *plane of the individual.*

Peter worked, probably still is working, very hard to make himself a *"place of comfort"* about his choice to exclude me from his life, also. For many years after we had acknowledged there was something *special* between us, but he wasn't going to do anything about it, every time I saw him, one of the first things he would inquire about was whether I had found anyone to marry, as though that should be my goal. I knew his conscience would feel better if he could visualize me, in this coupled world, in a more acceptable, not so lonesome life style. I also knew he was watchful for any information, which could allow him to trivialize our love so he could more thoroughly believe what the church taught him. Finally, after the umptenth time of this deceitful, mind manipulating, straight from the bowels of the *pep-fests for the celibate life-style* (better known as *retreats* to support the parish priest) tactic, I confronted him. I stated there was no possibility of that happening with my feelings where they were, especially since I was aware I couldn't force my body to cooperate.[5] He did not allow me to know his reaction; he did not attempt to correct me; he did not tell me I was being ridiculous because my feelings were inappropriate, or I had to try and move on as he had; he did not tell me his feelings for me had been misinterpreted; but, he has not attempted such a manipulation since.

Why aren't Pope John Paul II and his cabinet of Cardinals more open to changing the requirements for the priesthood? Their minimal dialogue about the reasons, with gapping holes, leaves us with one option; all we can do is hypothesize. I want to believe their intentions are good. Therefore, could there be a reason many of them aren't even aware of, causing them to have such strong opinions and feelings about keeping the celibacy requirements? I am sure what I am about to share has some affect in their choices. How much? is the question.

What is the average age of these gentlemen, these princes of the church? Over 65? maybe even over 70? I have had contact with aged and dying people all of my life and there are many common denominators. During the sixteen years as a nurse on a hospital trouble shooting team named Flying Squad, some weeks I was involved in a death a day, for weeks at a time. The biggest, most common joy for the aged is their children and grandchildren. Many times, the only regret they feel to the point of tears, when they know their death is eminent, is leaving the grandchildren and not knowing what the grandchildren will be like as adults. Otherwise, with their present weak and painful bodies, irretrievable love losses (parents, siblings, friends, etc.) there is nothing in this world worth *staying for.* When mental alertness and privacy allow, another frequent awareness the dying share is the "*love of their life*;" in some situations it was more like the dying had a *drive* to share the "*love of their life.*" In at least three of my

---

[5] See description of physical responses in pseudo-in love, page 57, 60, 61, & 67.

experiences, the *love* was socially unacceptable so they shared in a way where the message was between the lines (their faces would light up like a light bulb if I said or did something which indicated I had heard their message). Even in their final moments of life, sharing about their *love* gave them energy; they enjoy sharing those happy moments, times when they really felt *alive*. I have never heard things like, "Oh, am I joyful I made president of a major company," (which would be equivalent to being made a bishop), or, "I made the million I wanted to," (which would be equivalent to building a parish or two or three). Yes, they talk about going home to God in heaven (they must save this part for the priest or minister!), but not as spontaneously, out of the blue, as the information about those in their life path who were an intimate love connection. Back to these gentlemen/princes, who **choose** to *not experience* the two most important things the dying have shared with me. It seems quite plausible, in these days of the *winter* of their years, the pain of their choices is being felt; they are unable to suppress/repress the pain any longer. If you had made sacrifices with such extreme ramifications, could you admit your sacrifices were in vain? So those, who have reality knocking at their door, experience a surge of energy to find anything and everything to support their celibate choice, in hopes of convincing themselves their choice was really not ***in vain.*** (We, the public, are just feeling the reverberations of those elderly attempting to validate their own choices, stay in DENIAL. *"The subject is not up for discussion."* They fear discussion for it may produce information that would destroy their denial.) And to compound the problem, the members of the brotherhood, who are caring for them, are younger and still naïve about the meaning of their choices, still overwhelmingly enthusiastic about their perceived *Godliness* in being celibate. For these elderly princes, correcting their caregivers (the orthodox younger priests and assayers of information) would be the same as cutting off the hands of the ones feeding you. No matter their persona, these elderly are fragile physically and are just as dependent on their younger members in the brotherhood as an aged parent is on their children. Could you, would you, believe **truth** was important enough to threaten your *support system* and the *support system* of your fellow travelers? I do believe allowing married clergy would weaken the existing support system of the aged celibate clergy, especially in Rome. And I believe they will do almost anything to prevent jeopardizing their care during their most vulnerable time of life, consciously or subconsciously. Fear distorts the senses. Their inability to see the **anti-God** elements of forced celibacy could be a response to a basic instinct, **self-preservation**.

Now, combine the aforesaid with a *subtle message* my father's presented perspective taught our family during the last days of his life. Here was a gentle, wise man; the man who hadn't *"whimped"* out of informing me of the tough realities of life, announcing his life had been very good; he wouldn't have done it any other way if he had been given a choice. His children (my brother and me) and his adult grandchildren would catch each other's eyes, in disbelief, at these words. This was the same man who had his will to live taken away secondary to the verbal, emotional abuse from his wife. Is our dread of being "pitied" so great that, overall, mankind chooses *denial* of past pains? Are our egos so threatened with the possibility of being remembered as a *"failed life"* we can't face, much less present, the truth? Could *"Golden year"* celibate clergy, especially those who have denied themselves the one they love, be presenting a false picture, as my father did, when they say, "This has been a very good life for me. I really value celibacy?"

Since my first hand experience with LLL and knowing LLL has crossed the paths of many, including our celibate clergy, I am aware for those celibates having had the experience there are bottomless pits of pain just below their veneer waiting to explode. These celibate priests literally CANNOT drop the rock (admit forced celibacy is against God), which would commence an avalanche of terror in an uncontrolled slide down the mountainside. The avalanche of terror is the pain surfacing from the awareness, not only did they sacrifice their children, they needlessly sacrificed their LLL connection, and they may have <u>contributed</u>, in a major way to some of the most repulsive sins in this world.[6] These men, whose intentions were to do <u>Good</u>, may not survive mentally intact at such an acknowledgement. No way can these law makers accept they unnecessarily (unnecessary for the salvation of their soul), sacrificed such a beautiful life giving condition and children of their own, they then would need to acknowledge they unnecessarily sacrificed the person who triggered the life giving force to surface in them, and/or they possibly contributed to the commencement of generational sins. No way can these law makers, the Pope and Cardinals, the Bishops and Arch Bishops, acknowledge to themselves, much less the public, their ultimate sacrifice was **IN VAIN**! The pain surfacing would likely take their, now fragile, life. It would be *God sent*, God inspired, and the answer to a prayer of many of God's people if, like C.S. Lewis acknowledged about his own discoveries and ambitions,

"I creep home wounded and bruised having given up all ambition.
Only then can one truly say,
'Thy Kingdom come, Thy will be done...,"

these princes could be humble enough to genuinely pray the <u>Lord's Prayer</u>, open to God's wants, not their own, and make their laws compatible with God's laws.

The format Rome has inherited **its** instructions on how to *sway the masses* to their way of seeing God is millenniums old. Jesus corrected much of what was erroneous, but some slipped through the cracks and remains on our doorstep. What has worked in the past to sway the masses is not going to work on a large scale now; we are no longer illiterate; we have read the Bible; we have sought and received help with relationships and learned from the experience(s). When observing the Roman Catholic Church's response to the abuse issues and their choices of what to release

---

[6] Combine John Bradshaw's teachings (page 73-74) with what is taught with the non-verbal messages of the Roman Catholic Church (pages 122-136) to see probable contributions to repulsive sins.

to the press, it starts to crystallize, they are not considering how well informed the general public is about the intricacies of intimate personal relationships, or now, how many individuals trust their own minds to tell them what is right and what is wrong, and are not going to accept erroneous beliefs, which contradict what has been learned, learned the hard way, through **their own** painful life experience(s). Like Oliver Wendell Holmes acknowledged, "The human mind, once stretched to a new idea, never goes back to its original dimensions." The American Catholic cannot return to mid-evil, pre Vatican II, Catholicism.

The above stated fact, "The human mind, once stretched to a new idea, never goes back to its original dimensions," should be an enormous warning for Rome about the *instant messaging, cell cloning,* and *information doubling/quadrupling world* this is, but evidently not. The princes continue to attempt to return to pre-Vatican II days. The princes are **SO** arrogant in a time when a *remorseful-for-their-sins* person would be attempting to repair the damage done because of his sins, these princes have accelerated their thirst to find and punish (denying individuals communion) public figures, who belong to any political movement conflicting with the church's teachings. **THE PRINCES SHOULD BE DENYING THEMSELVES COMMUNION FOR THEIR SINS!**

Who will be the first to do a thorough investigation (spending contributed dollars) to find *stones to throw* at me for printing what is between the covers of this book (instead of paying penance for their sins)? for publishing this book?

You have just made an educated hypothesis, a prophecy, of sorts!

If the Roman Catholic Church is to have any credibility now and in the coming years, save itself, the hierarchy will need to acknowledge the enlightenment of the mass conscience and edit their laws accordingly.

The pedophilia, which so far has mainly been reported in the United States Catholic Church, is only the *tip of the world;* children are only the *tip of humanity.* Every man and woman throughout history, who have gotten close enough to recognize *Christ* in each other (God, Jesus Christ and the Holy Spirit are ONE), but can not traverse the abyss to actualize the recognition because *tradition* has erased the road, they and their children (each, then, united with a socially acceptable partner, not their LLL partner), are victims of Roman Catholicism. Each of these pseudo-*in love* unions have the potential of adding members to society with altered sexual triggers. It is no wonder, then, the number of reported cases, without considering the number of possible unreported cases, is overwhelming. From 1983 to 2002, Catholics for a Free Choice[7] compiled a thirty-one-page report of individual cases of priest/child abuse reported in newspapers around the world. Their footnotes document the name of the newspaper and the date(s) the information appeared. When assessing the information one needs to recognize, the freer the press is in any given country, the more documentation there will be. Another issue needs to be combined with the *freedom of the press* issue, the degree of freedom each individual citizen's mind needs to feel and have to openly acknowledge such deeds happened to him or her. In many cultures the degree of loyalty to the Catholic Church remains so high the victim feels as though they, themselves, are the guilty party and have not yet risen above their perceived sin to report incidences to the authorities. (Alone, the awareness the victims erroneously suffered and then, Rome added to the victim's suffering with their reflex action to cover-up their sins [many legal cases with *Silence Clauses* were settled out of court for large sums of money, in order to insure their secret would remain a secret], should *curl the hair on a moral, sensitive person's head.*) The victims in countries rich with loyal Catholics may also fear being chastised by those they care about if they should come forward. My first cousin, who lives in Minnesota, put down

---

[7] You can find this information on the internet at www.VOTF.com

a person for taking a priest to court. This loyal to the Roman Catholic Church versus loyal to TRUTH, resides right next door! From 1983-2002, there are twenty countries that have reported cases in their newspapers of priest /child molestation. As of 2002, the countries reporting the largest number of cases are: United States (304), Ireland (15), England (7), Mexico (14), Brazil (14) and Canada (10). The numbers emphasize three issues:

1.) The United States has the freest press.
2.) Many, many countries have a huge number of *Catholic loyal* vs. *truth loyal* citizens.
3.) Since 2002, many more have been reported in the Catholic dominated countries, validating the difficulty/pain of conflicting with Catholic Orthodox loyalists.

The other countries mentioned were Argentina, Australia, Belgium, Bosnia, Chile, Colombia, France, Germany, Italy, Philippines, Poland, Scotland, South Africa, Trinidad and Tobago.

I feel I need to reinforce over again and again, everyone in these reported cases is a victim of the belief system responsible, the Roman Catholic Church, including the abusive priests. (This is why the legal action, though absolutely necessary, makes me very sad.) We cannot deny *something* happened to these men in their formative years, which ideophrenicly[8] altered their internal triggers for sexual arousal. What confuses me is these men act like their behavior is *normal;* they almost look like they are confused why everyone is so upset about what they have done to betray the children. When the *powers in control,* who are the ones determining punishment, will excommunicate a priest who marries, but allows a pedophile priest to stay in the church, the *powers in control* are giving the non-verbal message, *"This is normal behavior."* When I consider the facts:

---

[8] Taber' Cyclopedic Medical Dictionary, author,Clarence Wilbur Tabor, F.A. Davis Company:
ideophrenic (id-e-o-fren'ik) Marked by abnormal ideas of a perverted nature.

- Rome excommunicates priests who marry, but not priests who have had sexual contact with minors, and
- the number of years (decades? centuries?) the Archbishops and Bishops protected the pedophile/homosexual priests, and
- the degree of duress the bishops endured from their flock and did not protect the children, much less, report these **betrayal of children** sins,
- only the legal action taken by the victims brought the information forward,
- only then, did the bishops own such crimes happened (only because they could not deny it any longer), and
- The Vatican promoted Cardinal Law, of Boston, to a higher paying position in Rome (which is announcing to all Catholic clergy, who follow Rome, we will protect you when you hide information for our image, and is slapping the victims in the face for coming forward with the truth as well as the judicial process of the United States).

My mind feels like exploding when considering the ramifications of the church's choices. My mind has to fight hard NOT to believe the hierarchy is secretly on the side of *evil*, the essence of the *underworld* at work now. (If not *evil*, Rome is surely anti-American! anti-democratic process! and Rome hates our free press for they must see truth as their enemy!) And they act like, "Oh well, we got caught, we'll do our petty penance, say we're sorry, and that's that." Even though their *petty penance* has turned out to be quite substantial - do you think they'll acknowledge it? No! "Everything is just fine, the people never lost their faith in us," they say. Oh Yeah? How many of you have had your faith in the church dented, majorly dented? But you had better not admit it publicly. (And you'd better not ask where the money is coming from to pay their legal fees all across the United States and now, the world.)

There are so many victims; not only are the priests, who cannot share life with their LLL connection a victim; the women, who are denied their *gift from God,* are victims; the priests who did the molesting are victims; and, of course, the child victims themselves (who, with no therapeutic intervention to attempt to heal the altered sexual triggers, will become adults, who will likely abuse children, and/or be homosexual). The number of people being victimized is phenomenal! All of the above are, most likely, those who really care about working for God in this world and these same caring people thought, believed to their *core*, <u>this is what they were doing by being entirely loyal to all Catholic teachings, doctrinal and traditional.</u>

God has been begging, "Please stop making the people who love God the most and will die to please God, God's Temples' victims." Only, God isn't saying, "Please!" anymore; God is demanding. For if the Church continues to stubbornly refuse to even discuss the Celibacy Laws; even after the hundreds, if not thousands, of lawsuits, negative publicity, rapidly declining chauffeurs, vocation shortages and last, but definitely not least, the awareness that THROUGHOUT HISTORY there have been thousands upon thousands of victims (considering the John Jay report revealed tens of thousands of documented cases back to 1955, the number of putative victims, throughout history, must climb into the millions!), who have NOT gone to court because they are too tired, old, sick and dead. The above doesn't even take into account the contribution of the sexual sins the church is responsible for, which aided in spreading HIV! (This is said in the light, which acknowledges all western Christendom originates in Catholicism) It hurts to consider what God will do next to coerce the hierarchy into change. Therefore, the Lord Almighty, the God of Israel says, "I will bring upon this city and her loyal supporters all the evil I have promised, because this city (the *Roman Catholic Church*) has stubbornly refused to listen to the Lord." *(Jeremiah 19:15)* For God wants the victims to know He hears their cry, "Spare me, Lord. Let me recover and be filled with happiness again before my death." *(Psalm 39:13)*

The Roman Catholic Church does have the correct laws about *how to find God's will for His people*, but these laws have been stacked in the wrong order of importance. In the realm of church teaching and law, let me clarify. First, everything in Catholicism, every law God gave us through Moses or Jesus, has been twisted and out right denied (Song of Solomon) to put the *plane of the community* first on their list of criteria to discern and promote what God wants from us. When it is individuals who comprise a community, how can this perspective be correct/Godly when this only allows the community to be as good as its best, but wounded and/or sinful person? With the existing priority of the laws of the church, the most spiritually refined are throttled and unable to accomplish their *God given goals*. The Roman Catholic Church needs to change its laws to support the individual **FIRST**. Only then are spiritually refined, spiritually unthrottled individuals able to contribute their God given special gifts to the community. *("Upon hearing this, all the powers of darkness tremble, Glory, Glory, Hallelujah, He reigns.")*

First, on the *plane of the individual,* no one can be fully productive when they are using their energy to deny God's will for them. When one believes the *community* is more important than the *self,* one won't even hear or believe what God is saying to the *self.* Even if this person is strong enough to avoid depression (no energy), this person is unable to love others as they love themselves because, in essence, they don't love themselves. A community where the individuals don't *love themselves* is a very dangerous community indeed; the list of the atrocities of what *man* has done to *man* in God's name throughout history is almost endless and is a testimony of the dangers.

Second, on the issue of celibacy, the church has all the vowels but refuses to use them (why?). Celibacy is pleasing to God, but only to adhere to HIS WILL for us, not to dictate to God what HIS WILL should be. It is innate in our being to be hungry for God to be in our lives, our life. On the *plane of the community,* the numerous religions around the world, with their lists of ways to be in God's favor, attest to this fact. On the *plane of the individual,* God's will for each of us to find who He intended for each of us to share life with, is so strong many of us actually feel hungry for the fruition of the seed God has planted in us; we want to be *in love* and in our impatience for God's will to unfold, combined with our naiveté, we misinterpret our feelings. Sadly, maybe too many of us find ourselves so hungry for the fruition of the God inspired *state of being*, unknowingly, because of withheld information, we *role-play* the experience as we imagine it might be and apply it to what is visible from our existing vantage point, in an existing relationship, and do all *in our power* to convince ourselves this particular relationship is the one God intended (in aggressively devaluing LLL, society overtly supports this approach to life).

"In our power" is no minor issue; many do quite a thorough job of convincing themselves they are, indeed, in love. When one is young, healthy, and energetic, deceiving the *self* comes with ease; self-*deception*, under the influence of exhaustion, disease, weakness and/or age is another matter; when inner *energy* is severely compensated or gone, the emotional misinterpretation will rear its ugly head. Without being consciously aware of the error, no tangible information to critique ourselves with and believing the joy felt at the commencement of their existing relationship was the result of being *in love*, God's people have made tragic mistakes in their choices for a mate. God's *timing* is illusive and needs all the TRUST-IN-GOD one can bring forth from ones core, ones soul, to travel where His will is. Traveling to *where* His will is for each one of us, to be pleasing to God, requires *celibacy* in route. **This end** needs to be the **work** of the church, what determines their laws, in order to be pleasing to God. God does not feel it is important enough to increase the population, thus power, of any religion by allowing, *encouraging with ignorance*, marriage and family for those not in a LLL relationship.

The ***joy,*** joyful *state of being,* that may be misinterpreted and used as a queue for labeling the existing relationship as an *"in-love" relationship* can be from various sources, i.e.:

-*the joy* at knowing you would probably have the babies you so desire,

-*the joy* of security, because you would marry into a wealthy family,

-*the joy* because of a possible/probable gain in status,

-*the joy* of believing you may never need to be alone again,

-*the joy* of having someone to share life experiences with,

-*the joy* of believing you are *visible* to someone, especially, if during your childhood, you were *invisible.*

-*the joy* of believing you can make someone happy, maybe someone with characteristics of someone, who, when you were a child, you weren't able to please, maybe one of your parents,

-*the joy* of intimately identifying with someone who emanates what you wish for yourself, but you have not or cannot accomplish.

-and all combinations of the above,

-plus, plus, plus.

The possibilities are almost as numerous as the individuals. To emphasize again, the *joy* experienced from meeting another need, combined with adolescent or young adult physically stimulated sexual desires, were mistaken for the state known as being *in love.* In my naiveté, for most of my life, I have believed that because we live in a *free society,* most couples, as well as I, had married for love, *in-love,* reasons. Whoa, not true. In our *free* society, the sad state of affairs is the aforementioned *joys* are the cause of too many erroneous marital commitments, mainly because our teachers have no skill, or are naive themselves, or they fear communicating what the *real thing* looks like. If it was *fear* preventing communication, mankind's history validates there *was* cause.

From the days of the Inquisition to burning witches at the stake, those in power have shown their distaste for the communication of the condition. It feels quite plausible the intense *fear* prevented communication for such a long period of time, generations, that when we achieved the freedom to communicate on the subject, we had actually forgotten how. And to make matters most difficult, the language needed to communicate it had been given a vulgar color, like the word lust, and we are reluctant to be accused of promoting *lust* (the expanded, erroneous definition most of us have absorbed)[9] to teach it. To totally describe LLL, *God, Jesus and The Holy Spirit* need to be referenced and doing this during Rome's adolescent years would have made one vulnerable to heresy charges and, if female, risk being burned at the stake. At least our society has a better chance than a society where the mates are chosen by other than the two involved (this would be another book if I could/would go there). Still, our *free* society has a long way to go. *Money* and power continue to support the perspective that devalues LLL. The *rich* are the ones who sign the paychecks of the employees of our communication systems (television, radio, magazines and newspapers), and are either naive or fear losing influence and power over their own young or spouse, so much, they want to hear LLL has no Godly value (it is amazing how hard we work to paint a picture that supports what we want to believe). Therefore, the *rich* choose those with anti-LLL perspectives for their self-help shows, articles and formalized psychology classes. Those, who promote anti-LLL, usually site several examples to support their perspective, but they never intricately investigate what the person, who claims to be *in love,* is really feeling or experiencing. Until I experienced the *real thing,* I would have honestly stated I had been *in love,* the feelings I had were all I knew. With the awareness I had made an emotional misinterpretation,[10] I am sure there are many, many others who have, also, and if they have not yet experienced the *real thing* or the misinterpreted relationship has not yet met an acknowledged insurmountable hurdle, they still believe their emotional misinterpretation is or was the real thing. At least the latter will

---

[9] See overview on the word LUST on pages 132-133.
[10] Refers to the *emotional misinterpretation* described on page 31 (mislabeled the *"joy"*).

say they were *in love* when they married, but believe ***it*** died. The lessons life experience has taught me is; these folks, even though they had the best of intentions, have erroneously labeled the ***joy*** they felt from other satisfied needs, combined with friendship and physiological sexuality, as the *in-love* Eros energy flow.

III
Love Knows

It has taken longer than God wanted, but I finally believe God hears me. The mighty miracles He has preformed day after day in my life, especially since 1989, rival the Book of Daniel, literally. Each day, if viewed alone, may not seem like anything other than a desperate person looking for relief from overwhelming pain; alone, each day probably appears more like a person who has lost contact with reality to stay alive. But when anyone, with any spirituality at all, views the consistency of God's messages to me, the truth of the prophecies He gave me and then manifested, and how His Words kept me from catatonic depression for more than ten years, will have a difficult time discounting the probability that God is the only answer to: "How can this be?"

It has taken longer than God wanted, but I finally believe what I hear in God's Words is what He wants me to hear. Talk about a *doubting Thomas*, this was me. I shouldn't be so *cocky* I say *doubting* in past tense, only; there are moments when *doubt* continues to overwhelm me. God doesn't take kindly to these moments. There is no, "Oh, how sad," or "poor thing," or "What can I do to help you feel better?" It's, "Son of dust, listen again to my words," and "Go to the Temple and announce..." and "Keep this up and you'll be the bones lying in the fields of unmarked graves." In the words of our day God is saying, "Pat, get your sorry ____ back in the saddle and go where I tell you before I have to punish you again."

It has taken longer than God wanted, but I no longer believe God is punishing me for *falling in love* with His priest, for God's will for His priest was both, the priesthood and union with his LLL other. For a long period of time God had to reinforce and reinforce, I was where He wanted me to be, before I could rise above my learned perceptions and acknowledge I had nothing to be ashamed of; I didn't cause it. LLL was God's blessing, who could feel ashamed of that? Objectively, who could be arrogant enough to refuse it? Refusing God's blessing would be parallel with handing back a valuable gift your Grandparents gave you with the air that it just wasn't what you wanted. Are the Grandparents happy you returned their gift to you, back to them? Are they happy it wasn't what you wanted? They had gone to a lot of trouble to arrange this valuable gift for you, and you felt ashamed of it – oh my. Looking at God's blessing from this perspective, I quickly changed my tune. My *learned perception and the feelings they precipitated* must be quite universal, at least among Catholics, for how many of the loves that priests have jilted are writing books to announce their plight? Not any! Right? The victims have been erased just as planned by the assayers of information and their *silent-treatment* plan of attack. Well, God has found a way around their roadblock. In order to relieve/lessen the pain of sexual sins around the world, mankind is going to need to acknowledge the importance of LLL, or succumb to a society which rivals the pagan society of the Spartans, 500+ to 400 BC.[11]

---

[11] Taken from the documentary, The Spartans, narrated by Bettany Hughes, a classical historian. The Spartan civilization, 500-400 BC, was militaristic, communal, disciplined, and a state that enforced eugenics and euthanasia. Priests would decide which babies should live and which should be left exposed to the elements on the side of a hill, to die. Their military was strengthened by a rarely spoken of life style, males were dissected from their mothers presence about the age of seven and adopted by an adult male warrior, never to live with his mother and siblings again. The adult male warrior was more than a parent to the child, he was the child's sexual partner. The homosexual tendencies were so strong that in order to increase their population, they incorporated into their wedding ceremony the tradition of shaving the female's head along with other changes to make her appear more boyish. The logic in this tradition is obvious; the husbands could not be sexually aroused by females after their sexual history with their adult male warrior parent. After marriage, the husband could live with the wife and children or continue living in the warrior brotherhood facilities, many chose the latter. One of the main reasons Sparta lost power was because of too few citizens and warriors secondary to their life style. This interesting documentary may be found in your public library. It is available in the Hennepin County Library, Minnesota.

THE FLYING SCROLL

It has taken longer than God wanted, but I'm finally to where I can communicate what has happened and is happening to me, in me and hopefully, around me. Never before have I felt the limitations of language so profoundly. In fact, the cavern between what I want to share and the picture words create is so huge, feelings of inadequacy bring me to my knees and tears of frustration to my eyes. (Dante's, Pilgrims Progress, comes to mind.) But the only choice I have is going forward, for dismissing God's command results in death, a death greater than the death of the body and the body, too. Ezekiel 6:14

God has worked very hard to keep me alive; keep me from the greater-than-death. For many years what I saw in His messages was a more eminent manifestation of His Words, more of a magic intervention. During those days, when God kept repeating and repeating He wanted Peter and I "together" and would accomplish getting us "together," I believed God would have us leave or be much less active in the Catholic Church in order to face life together. During those early years of surviving only because of God's Light, there was signal after signal in the news of the day what the Catholic Church taught, some verbally, but mostly with non-verbal language, was an erroneous perception of women, of intimacy, sex, and, especially, Life Light Love. The evening news was only reporting the ramifications of believing what the church was teaching[12] with their non-verbal language. Alone, this awareness was enough to keep me from feeling guilty about wanting Peter out of the priesthood, but then God told me of His anger at this idol (forced celibacy in the priesthood) worship, while continually reinforcing, if I was going to have any peace with Him, I had to make public what my life experience has taught me. So now I am on the opposite end of the spectrum from guilt; now, I need to launch a

---

[12] Please take time to read, Examples of What the Non-verbal Language the Roman Catholic Church Teaches, found on pages 122-136. This information will give you the vantage point from which the words on this and other pages are written.

rescue mission, a rescue mission, hopefully, to save many from making vows that, literally, block God's will.

There are so many insurmountable mandates from Rome defying the minds of God's people I couldn't stay active in the Roman Catholic Church without feeling totally hypocritical so I became inactive. Because of the Catholic Church's history of resistance to change, which has increased under Pope John Paul II, leaving the church actually felt like the holy thing to do. What preempted this awareness and decision was when Rome announced their money would be taken away from Catholic Colleges if their theologians were not teaching what supported Canon Law, artificial birth control was not even up for discussion and the era of **no dispensations** if a priest discovered God wanted him elsewhere, began. In good conscience, I could not and cannot support a religious earth bound institution, who closes its doors on God's people like that; I couldn't, until Gods' message made it through to me that He wanted me to help bring the church back to Him by writing this book. Since it was just a few years ago the church acknowledged Galileo's discoveries, I can't imagine I could write anything which could or would have an impact on the church, but God is giving me no choice, so I'll follow whether or not the *impact* does.

In this same time frame, because of the advice Peter had given me about situations in my life, I believed if I could see the *anti-God mandates* from Rome, so would he. And I believed he would *need to* change the path he had chosen, as his advice had caused me to do, in his life in order to live a non-hypocritical life style as Arch Bishop James P. Shannon[13] had done. But as God has repeatedly reinforced recently, God does not magically neutralize our free will[14] to accomplish His purpose. Peter decided to

---

[13] Please reference Bishop Shannon's book, The Reluctant Dissenter, about his life and fight with his own conscience. He questions, will I answer to God for living according to what I believe or will I answer to God for living according to what the Roman Catholic Church teaches?

[14] For a more complete understanding of free will, one needs to read When Bad Things Happen to Good People, written by Harold S. Kushner.

remain active in the Roman Catholic priesthood and to do whatever it took to be loyal to the church and to his vows.

My conscious mind was not totally shocked Peter chose to ignore our "blessing" and remain in the active priesthood, but my core (maybe sub-conscious?) was totally taken by surprise and devastated. *"To the core"* is where NON-VERBAL communication goes versus verbal. Verbal or written information leaves us a choice of whether to accept or reject the content; but, when one is not consciously aware of what action is causing what response, non-verbal communication doesn't give us a choice. My core had absorbed Peter's non-verbal communication completely; and, when his being didn't follow through with his messages, my insides were screaming, "default-default-default," and totally disoriented me. I had to travel through the mourning process before I could get myself *back* again. I'm still not sure all of me has returned; the discrepancy between his non-verbal messages and his decisions (what he verbalized to never contacting me to moving far away) are so great.

Peter bucked God's directions completely; he is completely compliant with the Catholic Church's clergy counselors and advisors to never <u>initiate</u> contact with me; the key word is *initiate*. His seminary training throttled the <u>initiation</u> of communication, whether via telephone, the US Postal Service or email. Since his personal counseling with traditional loyalists of the church, he has traveled from a man who would send a *thank you note* for a birthday card and giving me a Galway Irish Crystal heart box with the Claddagh Ring[15] symbol embossed on the cover to a man who refused to acknowledge the death of either of my parents with a note. Peter seems to have an intense desire to **want** to believe and be pleasing to church authority and this desire has him grasping at straws

---

[15] The history of the Claddagh symbol per the brochure that accompanied the crystal heart container with the emblem embossed on the cover: "The history of the Claddagh Ring goes back over 400 years to a small fishing village nestled on the shores of Galway Bay. Here the ring became a token of love, friendship and fidelity, when a seafaring Spanish Goldsmith fell in love with a girl from the Claddagh village and crafted the first Claddagh ring for her. Since that time the Claddagh Ring has become a symbol of love throughout the world."

in his attempts to devalue male/female relationships, including marriage and including us. (And this is scary stuff as the homosexual choir director would do the same thing; is the required, one needs routine scheduled *retreats* or drugs to survive, mandatory, and forced celibate lifestyle that close to the homosexual lifestyle?)

To an objective observer aware of these goals, the desire to **want** to believe, but can't completely, those he wants to emulate; some of his attempts were really a "hoot," they were so far from what was possible or probable in a given situation and, even though, the *out of context* remarks left me staggering in confusion. The first time I became acutely aware of this desire of his, in the middle of a conversation about the pleasures of his last vacation, a cruise, he interjects, referring to a man and woman traveling together, that he couldn't imagine what married people could find to talk about during an extended vacation. Can't you just see a man in his forties and a couple retirement age celibates basking in the sun on the deck of a cruise ship, having trouble trying to find something interesting to converse about, validating their choices with a quip like this about marriage? Maybe his viewpoint is what it is, because any vacation he's taken, outside his immediate family, has always been taken with those where he had to initiate the topics of conversation, to keep a conversation going, for he likely has been the caretaker host of his fellow elderly traveler's vacation events. (Yes, it feels quite probable he was honed from birth for the priesthood.) In this moment, in addition to seeing his conscious "*want*," it dawned on me how absolutely clueless he was about what shared moments with a significant other could, would and do entail. Peter is much more aggressive, when communicating via the written word, than face to face in conversation. In fact, with his written word it is nye impossible to miss his message. My head is still shaking in disbelief at how he utilized an automatic advertising promotion (a dating service) of an email server to let me know he thought it was great for me to have signed up, when such a possibility was/is the furthest from my mind and he knows it. Even though I have tuned into his message, "don't anticipate

THE FLYING SCROLL

a relationship with me," to this day, the *volumes* spoken with unintended, non-verbal messages, canNOT be erased. What also contributes to my believing the spontaneous non-verbal messages (most given from the subconscious mind, which cannot lie) more than what *abandonment* says (*abandonment* is a conscious, voluntary choice), are God's messages. For example, the messages God points out to me in the Bible tell me Peter is *filled with joy* in my presence and *joy* is exactly what he emanates after he realizes I am in his presence. (The message and the outcome match.) I've even been aware of parishioners at the same service being aware of his changed demeanor from *getting the job done* to a *joyous presence* in the moment, but they don't know why. I sadly acknowledge, he <u>wants to believe</u> the *joy* he emanates in my presence to be from his present life style (I've seen glimmers of anger that he is so joyful in my presence) and prefers the parishioners believe this, also (for the promotion of vocations).

Joyful moments are a divine treasure and many times those moments are contagious. During one of the rare times Peter and I met for lunch, we were *caught up* in *catch up* talk, while the waitress was attempting to do her duty and watching us to determine if we were ready to order. Upon completing the order, she looked at us with a wry grin and shared her observation, "Boy!" she said, "sure can tell you two are in love." Stunned by her intimate sharing of information, accurate observation and frank honesty, we just starred at each other wide eyed until our laughter took over. The waitress had hit the target dead center. She would have really grinned if she had known Peter was a Roman Catholic priest and after devouring a steak sandwich, announced he had even forgotten it was Ash Wednesday. I'm still shocked a priest, any priest, could forget it was Ash Wednesday, whether *in love*, or not!

I have given Peter ample room to tell me he does not love me, but he refuses to tell me that, too. If he had spontaneously, appropriately responded to one of my attempts to connect with him by verbalizing or writing me with the message, he does NOT love me, I would not/ could not be writing this book.

After our most intimate contact, yes he broke his vows,[16] God wouldn't allow me to open doors to anyone else entering into my life; I have been celibate since. Not only God's words to me forbid it, but the *happenings* in my life, very tangible interventions by God. The least subtle intervention by God was when I was visiting my mother for a weekend in my hometown (population about five thousand) a few months after the death of my father. Since Mom was an almost impossible person to please, before arriving at her house, I had decided I would do my best to make our time together as pleasant as possible by following her wishes and going wherever she wanted. After a full day of this approach, she decided we would go out to eat for the evening meal after the Saturday evening Mass. When she suggested a place, I went there and then she would, in an irritated voice, change her mind and direct me to go somewhere else. This happened four times; I amicably went where she pointed. Between destinations, she continually complained about how bad the food is everywhere. When we finally finished the meal at the fifth choice, she commenced badgering me because I wasn't talking to her enough. The *badgering* continued as we drove to her house and as she entered her kitchen through the door from the garage. Once she was safely inside I interjected between her complaining thoughts with the announcement that I was going out for a while and would return in a couple hours.

I drove directly to the only bar in town, the VFW and ordered the stiffest, palpable, drink I could think of, a Brandy Manhattan (Peter likes Manhattans and scotch, too). This particular drink was such a rare request everyone around the bar perked up and took notice. In the middle of the buzz about my drink, the leader of the band scheduled to play that night, approached me. His line was he wanted to know more about a lady who ordered such a drink. If I recall correctly, he was a teacher and the band was a sideline job. Our conversation was pleasant and easy. I was in desperate need of some form of *pleasant* distraction so, when he suggested

---

[16] Our LLL was consummated on September 13, 1992.

THE FLYING SCROLL

a cruise around town (it would take all of ten minutes!), I accepted with the condition I telephone Mom and let her know I was going to be longer than I had said I would.

This is when Mom informed me the police from my metropolitan suburb had called her looking for me. The *Breakfast Bandit,* as this particular thief had been nicknamed, had broken down my front door and, thanks to a neighbor, was captured in the process of deciding what to steal from me. He was armed with a knife so, "Thank you God," for sending me to Mom's for the weekend! (The capture was televised the next night and I wondered, but never discovered, if Peter had seen the broadcast). The police were planning to nail my front door shut and were wondering if I could gain access through the garage when I arrived home. Being I had been thinking, throughout my whole conversation with the director of the band, "God told me not to be with anyone but Peter; what will God do with this?" when I became aware of the news of the break-in and considered the *timing* of this news, I felt totally ashamed of not complying with God's directive and doing what I wanted. I couldn't exit the situation fast enough. When I relayed the news of the break in to the leader of the band as my excuse for not being able to follow through on my agreement for a ride around town, he had to wonder about the truth of it, the excuse sounded so outlandish. I graciously accepted a piece of paper with his telephone number, but never called him.

The shocking revelation of how serious God was about me being true to Peter super glued in my mind a message I can never negate, no matter where God leads me; I needed to follow or the world would devour me *lock, stock and barrel/ spirit, mind and body.*

It appears what God has shown me to keep me *in line* with His will, is exactly what is happening to the Roman Catholic Church; God is telling them the world will devour it lock, stock and barrel, if they continue to refuse to hear God's message, are ignoring it, or both. The number of God's people the church has injured must be staggering for everywhere I turn there is someone wanting to share their pain.

PAT HOCKEL

And today, June 22, 2003, Bishop Harry Flynn, "Holy Harry," with his intricately articulated words continues to say the church will recover from the sex scandals without any further adjustments in the church's laws. All around him at the Bishops Conference were their victims, in pain, desperately crying for help and a progressive change in the church, not a regressive change as all indicators from Rome verify. (They are regressing back to aggressively implementing their conservative orthodox mandates, which caused all the sickening sex sins in the first place!) There is no mention the injuries are so numerous it might be a good idea to investigate what was wrong with their system to *produce* so many abusers. No! They just reinforce the abusers will be removed from any position having contact with children. The Roman Catholic Church refuses to acknowledge they are responsible. For throughout the generations (a result of their patriarchal system, celibacy requirements, and their non-verbal messages), I wouldn't be surprised, if they are responsible for 99% of the deviations in sexuality in the Christian world. Through numerous generations, the seeds against God's plan have been growing and time has clouded the perpetrator, but not totally. The Roman Catholic Church is relying on the *cloud* to save it and are ignoring there are intelligent, very spiritual souls who have purchased *Infrared Vision Goggles*, who clearly see the church hierarchy sitting in the middle of their cesspool covered with gooey, smelly, brown gunk declaring, "There is *no shit* anywhere, our ideals are pristine!"

Time is on God's side. When God cared enough to send the Breakfast Bandit after me to prevent me from going against His will, I cannot fathom what He has in store for the Roman Catholic Church to save His flock from their anti-God laws. Whatever it is, we will all stagger from the fall out.

We've all heard it or the likes of it; we only *fall in love* with who we can't have, or we only stay in love because the relationship isn't allowed constancy for, when the two do experience constancy, we are told, the *high* dies. Whenever I inquired about "What is being *in love?*" from the sources available to me (the church, parents, friends with religious training, and relatives, who believed they had religious training), this was the only description of this life altering force they would put into words. This aspect of life is confusing to many, many people. Even my father, when relationship trouble was hurting him or someone he loved, would walk around announcing over and over again, as an exclamation, "What is love anyway? I don't think I know!" Even to the day he died, he hadn't answered his frequently asked question. The subject is so full of pain individuals can't seem to expand on it enough to allow the communication of a clear picture. Not until my inner energy had dwindled and I was no longer able to support the mask I had designed, did I realize something huge was being erased from the consciousness of mankind. Could this be an explanation of why the only observations people are able to share are much, much too simple? brain damaged simple? retarded simple? God didn't and doesn't want His people to stop there and relinquish their search for **"truth!"**

Before I made the marriage vow, I was neither presented with nor found any criteria emphasizing the importance of erotic sexual desires being present in a relationship as a criterion for marriage. There was no written material available communicating *in love's* erotic nature in a *holy* context, in a *God's Word* context or maybe, *God is trying to tell you something when it is present*, or NOT present, context. The only tangible, erotic elements of *falling in love* available were communicated in a lustful, sinful context. In fact, **LUST**[17] IS THE ONLY PERSPECTIVE I HAVE EVER HEARD THE CHURCH USE IN REFERENCE TO EROTIC SEXUAL DESIRES.... If people do think of the erotic sexual desires of *falling in love* in a holy way, they sure do keep it to themselves! There were no messages of, "Beware, when you are considering marriage, if erotic sexual desires do NOT exist."

---

[17] Please reference pages 132-134, for a more full reflection of the ramifications of the word, LUST.

During annulment classes given at the University of St. Thomas, in the description of a Sacramental Marriage (from the Theology side of the church), there were many elements of LLL described (i.e., emotional visibility).[18] By then, I was pleasantly stunned to have such information in print through the church, but the pleasant surprise was quickly erased when they emphasized these elements probably only happen after enough pains of life have been lived through, together. THIS IS ERRONEOUS, MISLEADING, a LIE and GIVING **FALSE HOPE!** The sacramental qualities the priest leading this class noted need to be present BEFORE MARRIAGE DECISIONS ARE CONTEMPLATED! Then used as an indication that the Sacrament of Marriage *is indicated* as an outward sign of what has happened on the *inside of* each making the vow, as every other sacrament is characterized, NOT, it will develop after time. Considering how vague and misleading the terminology is in this arena to begin with, my *gut feeling* is their research on the characteristics of a seasoned marriage couldn't adequately measure the ONENESS that was present when a couple made the decision to marry. Therefore their conclusion, surviving much pain together causes ONENESS, is misleading. (How many couples do you know or have you heard about, who separated because of the death of a child? Pain doesn't increase or cause a couple's inter-relational skills to improve.) **The couples seen as having a Sacramental Marriage in their Golden Years could have survived the pains of life because the ONENESS, as in LLL, was there from the beginning.** We can NOT ask too often, "Why did the church change the format (an outward sign of what the Holy Spirit is accomplishing on the inside) it utilizes for the sacraments, for the Sacrament of Marriage?"

In the fifth grade sex education classes of a Catholic grade school, my two daughters received an intricate physiological account of the sex act, much more intricate than the public school system of those days. The description was so intricate it was made mechanical, so intricately

---

[18] See footnote no. 26, on page 73, Emotional Visibility.

shocking their explanation seemed an attempt to burn the condition away before *feelings* could become part of the equation. To qualify the information ethically, of course, there were repeated exclamations reaffirming it is meant for married people only, but nothing about the messages *feelings* are trying to tell you. In fact, the message of the class was to discount any message *feelings* provide. This isn't the message when information is provided in hopes that some of those listening will choose a vocation in the church. As a people we have discounted feelings so much we all to often can't even correctly identify what we are feeling.

Discount feelings? I had received this message; and in my adolescence and young adulthood I did discount them. Ignorance causes pain; *pain causes growth.* The pain resulting from believing what is *dead wrong* about *feelings,* has caused me so much growth, I need to document what I have learned, hoping all this pain and growth aren't in vain; I am hoping others can be spared what I have gone through. If the only message you receive from this whole message is, "Hey, there's nothing wrong with me because I'm not sexually attracted to so and so, or anyone at the moment," the efforts to write this book are worth it. This acknowledgement will give your "self" permission to use your energy for more positive contributions to the world. But remember, LLL may be around the next corner and when/if it arrives, LLL will need your full support to survive this world's weapons. The only plan worth physically dying for is God's plan.

God is communicating with us continuously and much of His language is feelings. When I was nineteen years old, even twenty-five years old, I didn't know the intricacy of the message system our ***feelings*** provide. I had actually worked at disregarding ***feelings*** in making decisions or erroneously identified important powerful ones. This wasn't a difficult feat, as I had plenty of practice numbing my *childhood self* to survive with a verbally abusive parent, and this way of surviving was supported by the information I received from Catholicism, which was the only external source of information available to judge the world from my vantage point (which is too true for many, many in this world). Catholicism smudged the already cloudy information more on whether feelings should be given any credibility. The church does acknowledge feelings as a valid source of God's desire for each of us in reference to being called to a vocation, but invalidates feelings, when they determine a call to the married life, when/if one has answered a call to a vocation. Therefore, the church left me with more confusing information about feelings, so my only choice was to survive as I always had, by ignoring them. I was so adept at *numbing* myself, I was able to suppress/repress[19] feelings to an extreme degree, so extreme I actually succeeded for twenty plus years to consciously ignore the significance of medical findings, which had been presented to me the first year I was married (I was twenty years old). My, then, husband and I were together two weeks after our marriage and then separated for nine months; he was stationed with the US military in Germany. Within two days of reuniting, after our nine-month separation, I was in the military medical system in Germany, being treated for bladder and Trichomonas infections. I hadn't even recuperated from the forty-eight hours it took to get there (military charter left a lot to be desired), or adjusted to the time change!

Trichomonas is a venereal disease, an STD (Sexually Transmitted Disease), as it is better known today. Considering my proven respect for intimate sex, I was a virgin when I married, I had definitely not been unfaithful so that meant only one thing; my husband had been unfaithful to me. (Thank heaven I had the degree of respect I did for sex in my early adulthood or much effort would have been spent trying to convince me and the rest of the world it was my fault I had acquired STD. With the

---

[19] From Webster's New World Dictionary
repress 1. to hold back; restrain; as, repress a sigh   2. to put down; subdue   3. to prevent the natural development or expression of; as, the parents repressed their child.   4. **in psychiatry, a) to force (painful ideas, impulses, etc.) from becoming conscious.**
suppress 1. to put down by force or authority; quell. 2. to keep back; restrain: as, to suppress a laugh. 3. to prevent or prohibit the publication of (a book, etc.) 4. to check the flow or discharge of. 5. in psychiatry, **a) to withhold from consciousness. b) the deliberate exclusion of an idea, desire or feeling from consciousness.**

situation where it was, it was so obvious I couldn't be convinced, the whole STD issue was made invisible, instead.) My mind couldn't/wouldn't accept his betrayal. Reviewing my history and the circumstances at the time, it makes perfect sense my psychological safety system had kicked-in full blast and prevented me from acknowledging reality. The husband (mine) denied any activity which could have caused the infection, but I now know there was NO other way to get it, no other way than infidelity or adultery, no matter how hard I tried to believe his claim of ignorance. Here I was in a foreign land, I had just spent all the money I had to get to Germany to join my husband, had no money for a return ticket, and my folks were fighting for every cent they had, so it wouldn't be fair to them to request money to fly home. Oh, there's more! My folks had not been pleased I married when I did, and my peers also thought I was using poor judgment. My ego could not accept I had been that wrong. It wasn't until after my divorce, eighteen years later, the full impact of the sexually transmitted infection sunk in. *Denial*, it is an insidious enemy. My subconscious knew the truth; through those years I could never fully trust my husband by sharing my whole self with him and the un-owned cause of the infection was a major factor.

As far as the feelings of what I had believed were *in love* feelings, when I married, after experiencing the *real thing* I now can see my errors were similar to calling a *car* a *semi-tractor trailer truck*, or naming a *bicycle* a *Greyhound bus.* Yes, they all have wheels, but, when you have ridden a Greyhound bus and a bicycle, you will never confuse them again; so it is with an emotional misinterpretation of romantic love versus the erotic, undeniable, *real*, romantic love, LLL. *Ignorance* of what feelings are what, in the realm of *Love,* is a WHOLE LOT OF IMPENDING, DEVASTATING TROUBLE. This TROUBLE did double duty on me.

The human brain works very hard to forget *pain* and resists re-calling painful aware nesses. When we are in fear of change, the brain will even go over the edge of the abyss by denying a particular situation is causing *pain* in the same way I denied *where* the venereal disease came from. I have grown out of the *denial* phase but, even yet, it is still painful to relive what brought me to the *transitional trough* in my life in order to document it, again. I did document this period of my life before, for the St. Paul and Minneapolis Diocese Tribunal. I was hoping I had done a thorough enough job then, so now, all I would need to do is transcribe what I had written onto those pages. But, even though what I could share at that time was sufficient for the Tribunal to annul my marriage (1987), it isn't sufficient enough to give an intricate picture of what needs to be understood in order to identify the true character of human erotic, romantic *love,* when God is in the equation, LLL.

I really am not comfortable going this *deep* into me; I feel suspicious no one will believe me; I'm not in favor of the general public knowing me intricately; I don't feel any more gifted than anyone else, so why would anything coming from me be given any credibility? (Are these feelings the result of living in a Patriarchal system?) These are the feelings embodied in my being which brought me back to God's Word, the Bible, to ask again, "Is sharing what brought me to the awareness of the importance of LLL what You really want me to do?"

"Yes, I demand it!"" was God's reply, and this reply was reinforced in the scripture readings and homily at church this morning. (September 28, 2003).

IV
THIS IS THE AIR I BREATHE

There have been numerous written attempts by *truth seeking* members of mankind to subtle convey to each other and future generations the character of LLL, so it can be recognized so, when one says, *"in love,"* the one speaking means what the one hearing understands. Thus far, mankind has failed. Subtle doesn't work in this arena. One person understands one segment of it and the other person understands a totally different segment so, when they try to make an all encompassing universal statement about IT, they end up praising the manifestations of IT that they are consciously aware of. It is likely neither one in the conversation is consciously aware of or willing to own the magnitude of the WHOLE; probably, because one needs to reference God, souls and angels to accomplish it and our brains have been so conditioned, centuries of conditioning, to have feelings of blasphemy or heresy, when putting *erotic love* in the same sentence as *God*. Or today, we may simply fear being accused of lust. The ultra rich and powerful have gained so much compliance from society, mostly through religions and playing on the *jealousy* seed in all of us to punish any owners of LLL, the negative possibilities are too many and so great, our minds won't even tempt trouble by going there.

The WHOLE of LLL is so huge it is overwhelming. I cannot add or subtract from the beauty of <u>The Song of Solomon</u>; I doubt anyone can. In fact, I need you to go to your Bible and read it before reading the following, for the following experiences were totally in the light of what is described there.

In the beginning of this condition there were several years of two to four hours of sleep a night, because all my senses were so turned on I couldn't shut them off. The sleepless nights, strangely enough, didn't seem to affect my alertness the following day. When I did sleep, many times I would wake up from a dream in orgasm for I was dreaming Peter was in me. After a time, when it became a fact Peter and I could not share time and space, I avoided sleep to avoid the dreams for I would wake up startled, my face wet with tears, and couldn't return to sleep for the tragedy of the circumstances. This change in life's momentum was a bit of a shock, to say the least, for in the past I didn't climax when I was having intercourse with my husband.

Nothing nullified my desire to have intimate contact with Peter, mental or physical. When I say nothing, I mean nothing, not pain (I started to wear a rubber band on my wrist and would snap it hard, over and over in an attempt to cut the thoughts and desires), masturbation, working so late into the night, sleep was the priority and, not even, the death of dear loved ones. In fact, the later made my desire for him worse.

Unannounced, a vision of his face pops up before me, or the sound of his voice echoes between thoughts. For years after I met and *fell in love* with Peter I had spells of what sounded like distant thunder invade my hearing several times a day. Either Peter's face popping up before me or his voice creeping in between thoughts would precipitate this *"thunder."* Since I have resigned myself to the fact there is no hope for us to be together, over the years these *thunder* episodes have diminished in frequency, usually one a day or every other day, usually just before I fall asleep. I find it intriguing that during these thunder-like episodes, I don't feel sexually aroused, but if my feet are cold they warm up, if my head or stomach hurt they cease hurting, and I can fall asleep. In recent years, I have come to anticipate as I retire for the night; when I hear the *thunder* and/or feel a low resonance vibration, it won't be long before I am comfortable and sleep will soon ensue.

When I first experienced this *thundering* phenomenon, I thought it to be a symptom of an injured brain, and hoped that time would heal the injury, and the *thunder* would cease. Much of me wanted my old boring *self* back. As I continued actively resorting to invalidating these low resonance vibrations, thunder, along came the movie <u>Passage to India</u> (1984-1985, but I saw it, probably, around 1986-1987). A young head strong British woman, engaged to the son of her traveling companion, agrees to allow a Muslim physician show her some sacred to their faith caves. When they are researching the caves a whole being thundering vibration engulfs them, as well as others who needed to be awakened to their truth, several times during several visits. Before any in the audience were aware of what was to follow, I thought, "Good grief – that's like what is going on in my being!" The plot of the story was rather slow and the ones I was attending the movie with were getting impatient for the plot of the story to unfold, NOT ME! I sat there wide-eyed, kind of in shock that what I was attempting to invalidate was being tangibly validated in the story. I was in shock; because, having this aspect of *the condition* on the screen meant mine wasn't an isolated case. A person never having experienced this *thunder* would have trouble tuning into the less obvious story in the obvious one, a conflict between the British and the local Indians. Whoever wrote the story has been there and whoever prepared it for the screen had experienced the *thunder*! From someone who was there, me, the message the story gave was, because the two had *fallen in love*, a tangible symptom being the *thunder,* she was feeling intimate, powerful sexual desires for the physician. But, the young British woman and the Indian physician were culturally so far apart the woman, in trying her best to deny her own feelings, actually accuses the Indian physician of rape – an absolute outlandish accusation according to the history in the story. But, the message deserves sobering consideration. On the plane of the individual, when we WANT to be seen as part of a certain class of people and culture and something happens that may threaten what we want, we will kill what is most beautiful to remain, in our eyes, where we want to be. This young lady could not commit to marrying her former fiancé after she fell in love with the Indian physician, but she abandoned the physician to live a single life rather than acknowledge her feelings for the physician to him or anyone else. (This scenario sounds like what Peter has done, yes?)

Being the *"thunder"* is valid, not just a sick symptom of my own mind, maybe the following is valid, also. About the same time I realized there was something larger than I ever imagined could possibly exist between Peter and I, I also noticed a very fine non-symptomatic rash-like character to the inside of my mouth. When I researched it out with a magnifying mirror, I could see there were thousands of the tiniest water blister-like eruptions just under the surface of the mucosa on the inside of my cheeks and lips. They didn't hurt; they didn't itch; they were not inflamed; other than my tongue being aware of their slightly different texture, they seemed completely innocent. My crazy brain thought, "Dopamine overload!" Six years after I met Peter, these almost microscopic blisters were still present. It wasn't until I had not had contact with Peter for over a year, they disappeared. These eruptions were such a minor change in the character of the mucous membrane, I'm sure if others have had them, they could have been totally unaware of their existence.

Between the two entwined in LLL, touch is, for the lack of another word, HOT. Even his hand on my shoulder left an area of glowing warmth after his hand was gone or the half-inch spot on the palm of my hand where his finger touched my skin as he laid the Host upon it. About the time I had consciously become aware of this phenomenon, I observed it was happening to Peter, too. During an after-service greeting, I had laid my hand on his arm. After I departed, I glanced back only to find him staring at the spot on his arm where my hand had rested. He was so engrossed with this area of his arm, when some other parishioners approached him to make conversation; they had to greet him twice before he could pull his eyes away from his arm to greet theirs. There's more than the glowing warmth, there's a confusing sadness when a *touch* ceases. It's like the area of touch had a huge *life giving* energy transfer, which stopped when the touch stopped, like so much energy passed through the small area of touch all the cells are hyperactive and glowing from the activity, and are screaming to retain the source of energy that bolted them into life. Since I have experienced this *touch*, almost every time I recall it, the ceiling of the Sistine Chapel in Rome pops into my mind. I wonder, did Leonardo Devince have this same experience and this energy flow was what he was portraying when he painted the life-energy of God flowing through His finger to the finger of mankind?

Before Peter, I had never experienced the desire to take everything of someone else inside me. This whole experience was uncharted waters. Not only did I desire to internalize his thoughts, words and actions, when we kissed I desired his breath, his exhaled air, of all things. Just being in the same room with him made me feel *breathless* like someone had sucked the oxygen out of the air and I had to breath deeper and faster to get some. Until *breathlessness*[20] happened to me, I had no clue what was being referred to in romantic songs or lyrics. Here I was in my late thirties and early forties, experiencing all these *firsts – wonderful firsts*, which were answering a lot of questions I didn't know should even be asked, in spite of the overwhelming pain *no hope* caused. I now have a whole new understanding to the lyrics of a love song, "All I need is the air that I breathe, just to love you." Goodness, before LLL I could never have imagined a vision of anyone's face popping up before me could/would cause breathlessness or eventually other orgasmic responses right in the midst of accomplishing activities of daily living.

---

[20] Is it coincidence that 'breathlessness', 'the air I breathe', 'you take my breath away', etc. are verses in contemporary Christian music? When LLL is God's blessing, it is no wonder the language, which describes God and LLL, are almost if not, identical.

Oh yes, a visualization commenced formulating in my mind of two cloud-like forms of energy, one representing Peter's spirit and one representing mine. These clouds, warmly and gently moved toward each other until they were totally submerged into one cloud, every molecule from one cloud intertwined with the molecules of the other. When the molecules from both clouds were completely intermingled as ONE, then the *one* cloud became a fireball of energy in mutual joy and gladness and orgasm. I suppose this visualization can be reduced to the *urge-to-merge*, but before I lived it, I never would have imagined, much less, experienced, such a visualization. In fact, a description of such a visualization would only have confused me and I probably would have dismissed such a thought as bazaar, I was so clueless.

Have you ever experimented with mirrors? Have you lined two mirrors up in such a way the reflections duplicate themselves indefinitely? to infinity? When Peter and I make direct eye contact this is what it reminds me of, to infinity, or more profoundly, like echoing the great *I AM*. Many times, to reach that place of *peace* in my soul, all I would need was a split second of eye contact with Peter. I didn't need to talk with him or touch him. A split second of *pupil to pupil* could give me enough energy to be productive for a couple days. Being consciously aware of this can be a *good* thing, especially, when one needs extra *life energy*, at any given moment to do *good*, like help my parents through their dying process.

This phenomenon is a more frequently documented happening throughout history. There are religions forbidding men and women, who are strangers or acquaintances, to make eye contact; Hinduism is one and the orthodox Muslim is another. Since I have experienced the power of it, it is no wonder those seeking to protect their worldly assets, in desperation, made laws against eye contact between the sexes so the recognition of a LLL other by their wife (wives in some cultures) could hopefully be prevented. Making laws to interrupt and/or prevent recognition of an LLL other is some insurance to these men, who made the laws and enforce them, that their wives won't find their LLL connection *(fall in love)*, threatening his ego and his household's peace, wealth or both; laws like no *eye contact between men and women* does help to insure these men are more likely to keep their property (their woman/women). This oppressive life style exemplifies how desperate man is to maintain and increase his wealth, how desperate man is to **be God**, rather than follow God. Blocking this energy that passes between pupils may be declared the equivalent to raging a battle against God, Himself. Who do you think will win – in the end?

The Roman Catholic Church is not naïve about the potentials of this *to the soul and beyond,* male/female *eye contact,* either. From a long lost article I jotted down the following:

Adverte oculos

It means turn away your eyes.

And that's all a seminary faculty member would have to say. They would walk past you and they would just simply say, 'Custody of the eyes."'

What I find equally fascinating is neither before, nor during, my annulled marriage did my husband and I ever make any extended eye contact. In fact, my *ex* would do almost anything to avoid eye contact. Looking back, this very likely could have been a manifestation of guilt (his adulterous behavior resulted in me being sick with STD) along with the absence of LLL. During our courtship, though, he also avoided eye contact so the absence of LLL must be the primary cause.

In the recollections of sexual feelings during my pseudo-*in love* marriage, before LLL found me, any desire for the sex act feels like it was a need for *touch* from someone who possibly cared combined with a desire for children. Eventually, my husband's response to various life experiences, time after time, had convinced me he loved our life style, his needs being taken care of, and our unit's image, NOT me. The power of needing *touch* and *wanting children* is nothing to sneeze at, but I was continuously striving to bury and negate the repulsive feelings of *those hands* (my husbands) intimately touching me. Burying these feeling (I didn't want them) consumed vast amounts of energy, energy that was no longer available as the years rolled by. So much energy, I resorted to having a good stiff drink (or two) to, again, push those repulsive feelings back to where I had buried them, whenever sex was solicited. He questioned me on why I never initiated sex with him; he had no idea how fortunate he was that I *could* participate when he was the initiator. There is no way my whole being, spirit, mind and body, connected in desire for union. Since my body was usually fatigued from activities of daily living, there was no residual energy, without the energy from my mind, to overcome the anti-intimate messages present in my being.

In pseudo-*in love*, the body leads the mind; in LLL, the mind/spirit leads the body. In fact, with LLL, the mind/spirit overwhelms the body with so much Light and Life; it feels like every cell is in balance with its neighbor for optimum performance for any and all things one attempts to do. (If I could empathize with God, I'd consider this a fabulous plan!)

Yes, the only language available to describe the feeling(s) present in me, when I am in the company of Peter, is ecstasy. It is an overused word so it, even, feels very inadequate. When I combined the definition given in a Catholic encyclopedia with the definition found in Webster's New World dictionary, the meaning comes closer to what the experience has been.

<u>Catholic Reference Encyclopedia,</u> Catholic Educational Guild, (1968 C.D. Stampley Enterprises Inc., Charlotte North Carolina.
ECSTASY: A state in which a man passes out of himself, i.e., out of his natural state of cognition. According to St. Thomas, ecstasy may proceed from bodily causes, i.e., disease, or it may be caused by an agency of devils, or it may come from the Spirit of God. If it proceeds from the Holy Spirit it is a state in which a person is withdrawn from the senses and raised to the contemplation of supernatural things. Such ecstasies are, of course, frequently mentioned in the Old and New Testaments and

THE FLYING SCROLL

have occurred in the lives of many saints. Mystical writers tell us that in ecstatic prayer, the senses are suspended, but the will, retaining its full power, is absorbed in God.

<u>Webster's New World Dictionary</u>

ECSTASY: 1. State of being over powered with emotion, especially joy. 2. a feeling of overpowering joy; rapture. 3. a trance.

It actually does feel like *ecstatic prayer* when interrelating with Peter, there is definitely over powering joy, both time and the senses feel suspended and I am definitely in a state of rapture. And, when I consider I am always (in my mind) talking to God about the moment, and God's responses are continuously tangibly manifested, this is a *"contemplation of supernatural things."* All moments in Peter's presence have some element of ecstasy present. Since the moments Peter and I have shared one on one have been so rare, when there is a moment of interrelating contact, I know the brevity of it and so find I can do nothing that could potentially spoil the moment. Despite the importance of God's will being manifest (blocking His will, LLL, will affect the health of His Temple, our bodies) I cannot aggressively confront Peter about his feelings and choices; all I have the strength to do is thank God for the moment.

As the years passed, there developed a routine of being in Peter's presence with all these feelings and then no contact with him for extended periods of time, I discovered a distinct pattern of feelings affecting my whole world. The day of contact followed by about two and a half to three days were filled with energy, productivity and contentment. But then commenced feelings which were paralyzing. My heart actually would hurt, I had no energy to accomplish anything productive, and I was vulnerable to any contagion that was around. This immobilizing pain lasted three to four days and then relented into a desperate ache, which lasted until I could see his face (pupil to pupil) and hear his voice again. This circle of feelings happened so many times I reached a point where I commenced a mini-scientific study. If I was feeling healthy and energetic, I would consciously check if my present state had anything to do with my last time with Peter, "Oh yeah, I saw him yesterday!" If I was having trouble accomplishing anything, sure enough, I hadn't seen him for a week or two. When it became apparent how I was feeling was so predictable with the time of my last contact with him, I tried to prepare myself for the *down times* by keeping myself super busy in business. This didn't work. The only activity, which did help, was praying to God, and even then, I couldn't always avoid the immobilizing pain.

There is another undeniable difference in feelings and desires between what I thought was *in love*, pseudo-*in love*, and the real thing, LLL. I was totally unaware this *place in thought*, wanting to do exotic things to his body and know his body intimately, could actually exist in my mind before LLL descended on me. Before LLL, when I discovered how some women pleased their man, I was "yucked-out." I couldn't believe a moral and healthy female mind would ever go as far as to want to contaminate her mouth to sexually stimulate her husband – or – I wondered if that couples relationship was on such shaky ground she needed this extreme behavior to help their relationship survive. It never occurred to me to ask myself, "Why would knowing my partner's body extremely intimately be a turn-off?" The only answer I have, even now, is I was not ONE with the person I married, never would be and therefore, I could not give that much of myself to him. (Now, even though it was not a factor for annulling my marriage, it feels even more appropriate that our marriage was annulled; since I have discovered the main requirement to define a Godly marriage, a sacramental marriage, needs to include, if not be, the LLL factor.) The thought of, intrusive thoughts of (I'm not consciously bringing the thoughts to the surface of my mind, they are just there!) knowing Peter's body intimately puts a warm glow on everything. Even as repulsive as I had imagined oral sex, oral sex would be only a part of the whole picture of *knowing him*, and the excitement caused in him would be the excitement caused in me, ONE. Now, all I can do is wonder whether this scenario would have played out in reality – but – I no longer believe it is an unhealthy or sinful mind, which participates in such activity in an LLL union. In fact, such desires and behavior, when it is induced by LLL, probably is a sign of an ultra healthy and moral mind; it is a total, uninhibited, giving of self and allows the self total vulnerability, a needed element for the actualization of what is happening in the mind and soul to happen in the body. There are possible dire consequences for role-playing that this degree of intimacy exists in the mind, when it doesn't. I do believe these dire consequences contributed to various promotions that to be *"holy"* one does not partake in such activity. Because there wasn't (and barely is now) language to define what *role-playing*, versus, *what reality is* in the arena of feelings, this, *over all*, perspective was, essentially, mandated. This view further smudges the picture of what an individual should give credibility to in the *"self."*

Shortly after the premature death of his wife, C.S. Lewis, who defied the patriarchal education system in England to marry a divorced American lady, wrote to a friend that there wasn't an inch of her he didn't know.[21] LLL has crossed many a wall, equivalent to the Great Wall of China, to be actualized. If you are planning to marry and the aforesaid sensuous descriptions feel foreign and don't make sense to you, you may want to reconsider your marriage plans. Lack of these described desires and feelings is a warning that you are not experiencing LLL. Marrying a *friend,* in the end, does not work.

Peter is unaware of the above being in my mind about him, or, is he? The ESP-like non-verbal communication said so much at times, I found myself stunned into silence too often.

The *idols* of the world (more money, more power, more land, more status) do fear LLL; they fear it so much the idol worshippers are almost *crazed* to prevent/annihilate/control LLL. One such *crazed* attempt to

---

[21] From the book, A Severe Mercy, by Sheldon Vanauken. Includes 18 previously unpublished letters by C.S. Lewis. Bantam Books.

accomplish the prevention of/ annihilation of/ control of is to non-verbally cause **no respect** for the largest group of individuals the idolaters fear, **the female portion of the population.** It's not that man fears females as much as it is *man fears LLL*. Not until credible documentation became available in the twentieth century to validate that *falling in love* requires interpersonal respect at a deep level in the whole person (mind, body and spirit), there wasn't even a **tool** to consciously acknowledge a probable ulterior motive for erasing the *"un-equal to man"* image of woman or to identify this as an anti-LLL, anti-God sin against an individual by the controlling powers in a society (thus putting another road block in place to prevent the actualization of LLL). Every religion on earth has non-verbal messages stealing *respect* from a woman in hopes of preventing the *ordained by God union* from being recognized by the man, who is more likely to have the power to actualize the union. The non-verbal message relayed in *"No female Roman Catholic priests allowed,"* (*TEACHES* us God does not respect woman as much as men and does not want women representing God/Jesus in this world; females are not *worthy*), alone, diminishes the respect of a female body AND soul so much, a man, who is aspiring to be very holy and who has *owned* (consciously or unconsciously) this non-verbal message, would rather sit in jail the remainder of his life than, as he perceives his situation, rather than <u>displease God by intimately connecting to a **less than most holy being**, a woman.</u> (This mindset has prevented the actualization of many, many LLL discoveries.)

Because of Vatican II, even the hope, in the future women could/ would be ordained, has allowed more *respect for women* to enter the souls of men, allowing more LLL unions to be realized. I consider this as possibly one of the reasons why Peter's heart, at least, heard God's messages about LLL and where he needs to put me in his life to have a fulfilling life, where he needs to be in his mind to avoid the prison cell with invisible walls. Also, the fact many female pastors in other Christian denomination have proven their Godly worth in the cleric role so successfully, many men are no longer able to discount the value of women to the degree that prevents men from recognizing or experiencing a LLL calling. A man has a better chance of no longer finding it repulsive, threatening to his ego, or ungodly to be spiritually, emotionally and physically ONE with a woman. It feels like God *snuck this piece it in* when patriarchal men weren't looking. This has been a HUGE silent step for the human race. However, the intellect of the Vatican has recognized the error and has voraciously commenced an attempt to erase it; the Pope and his College of Cardinals are relentlessly trying to erase the message(s) of Vatican II, from the most recent <u>Theology of the Body</u>[22] (concentrates on the different roles of men and woman ingrained from body to soul,[23] to emphasizing how pleasing the Vow of Chastity is to God), to regressing to the pre Vatican II vernacular of the Mass.

Diminishing the value of the WHOLE "*self*" diminishes the possibility of LLL being recognized and actualized. Rome is reinstating pre-Vatican II language, while attempting to make their move appear progressive versus regressive, to the vernacular of the Mass. "And God be with you," will be changed to a more direct translation of Latin (as they want us to believe), to "And God be with your spirit.'" With this change, Pope John the II is recalling any personal *respect*, to the core *respect*, for EVERY individual that seeped out of Vatican II. The "you" in "And may God be with you," includes the whole person (mind, body and soul), whereas, "And may God be with your spirit," excludes your mind and body. After a person has repeatedly chanted the revised ("with your spirit"), the vision in the chanters mind will gradually change to exclude any personal

---

[22] For an insightful overview of Pope John Paul II's, Theology of the Body, see The Catholic Spirit, January 29, 2004 issue. This issue may also be retrieved and accessed at www.thecatholicspirit.com.

[23] The men who formulated the Theology of the Body are men who want their power back, men that want to enhance their ego by putting women beneath them in their perception of God's plan. (They emphasize the word "different" to take the obvious sting out of their message.) Like all non-verbal, manipulative messages, truth is kneaded in with deception to a degree where a person has great difficulty "separating the thistles from the wheat.'" Be careful what you, God's child, own from the whole (verbal with non-verbal) message found in Theology of the Body, or you may become a victim of prevented/annihilated/controlled LLL, as Peter and I are.

mentally induced conclusions, and presents an image of the body devoid of sexuality. Our *Temples of God,* our minds and bodies, do not deserve this disrespect. God, then, does not deserve this disrespect; He made us in His image and likeness. Does the Roman Catholic Church want Catholics to return to the same mental status that allowed Hitler to kill millions of people, without lifting a finger to prevent it? The Catholics of Germany were so accustomed to **not asking questions and following what was preached from the pulpit** (not using their own brains)**,** only, it didn't cross the minds of the average parishioner, then, to do anything about Hitler. Mankind will perish if it returns to that or a similar **mindset.**

(Now that I can see how desperately important it is to the ultra wealthy to kill any tangible knowledge of the importance of LLL, I wonder if Rome, in its present monetary decline, has been bribed with a very appealing *carrot(s)* to revive pre Vatican II days.)

Being conscious of what has been done to the image of women in man's eyes to prevent, devalue and kill LLL, my awareness has evolved to where I can form the language to communicate the missing piece of the trillion, no zillion piece puzzle. This piece is, every religion with GOD and GOOD as its primary focus is teaching us where to look for *"God's will"* for us. That is, every religion after one forces its' beliefs through a sieve to remove any elements of:
- "We are the only way to God"
- verbal or non-verbal messages that loyalty to its beliefs and community is more important than **TRUTH** and following the Ten Commandments or the like thereof, and
- any hint of an idea supporting one human having more value than another in God's eyes (from racial prejudice to *no* woman priests to the radical treatment of woman in the Middle East).

After these <u>anti-God elements</u> are removed, what remains is a path leading to where genuine *in love* is, God's will for His people's life experience. These <u>anti-God elements</u> are greed and power talking. (Has the human race commenced, with God's help, separating the thistles from the wheat?)

So, most of you, who are reading this, already have the foundation of the message I have been catapulted into giving. Hopefully, a few of you have consciously traversed the *abyss* from the foundation to living in God's Light (like C.S. Lewis), but I doubt your numbers are numerous.

Of course there are some religions that have a better-lit path to follow God's will than others. This does NOT mean the paths that are at dawn or dusk are wrong, it only means it is easier for the person following the well lit path to get where his/her soul wants to go, get there faster and increase the chances he/she will *get there*. Jesus Christ honed, bulldozed and cleared a well-lit path through the jungle, and those, who follow His path, are quite lucky they inherited and/or chose this clearer route.

Because the Roman Catholic Church has the accepted, essentially correct beliefs, but have them stacked in the wrong order of importance, when being presented to the people, it causes God's path to drop off into a bottomless pit with NO escape, I often find my mind comparing this moment of revelation with how a mother must feel when she discovers her son just murdered someone; and if she doesn't call the police to have the son arrested, it's most probable he will kill again. Dialing 911 to report the whereabouts of her son, must be one of the hardest things a mother would need to do. This is *where* I find myself in relation to the Roman Catholic Church, not *revenge*. Therefore I need to clarify; because the relationships most of us see are those based on pseudo-*in love* (which requires gross amounts of energy to maintain, stealing *life energy* from doing *good*, versus LLL, which gives life energy to do *good*) it can easily be understood the intentions of most of the law makers and assayers of information in the Roman Catholic Church, could believe ***forced celibacy*** is pleasing to God (to the ultra conservative, orthodox Catholic), or tolerated by God as a means to what they perceive as a better end result (to a liberal Catholic, but CATHOLIC). In other words, these vowed may have been raised in a home with parents who were a painful example of marriage; their parents had married for pseudo-*in love* reasons. These *vowed* have also mistakenly made choices with incomplete, misrepresented information. In this context, there can be forgiveness in my deepest core where the injuries took place, **when/if they change their traditional perspective, which will necessitate changing their laws.**

Thanks to a free press (or we would not have heard about the actions against the church for their *betrayal of the children* sins), human rights and human rights activists (they made it more comfortable so more of the victims could come forward), our judicial system (even as flawed as it is) and a vastly literate society (we have been literate long enough to know we can and do trust what our minds deduce), we, God's people, have more information to discern that the all encompassing, total life commitment to celibacy laws, with no exceptions, is anti-God.

Yes, we are to be celibate, but in the context it applies to every relationship outside of the one *ordained-by-God*. "**Ordained by God**" then becomes the issue, yes?

On the plane of the community, Roman Catholic hierarchy have done a thorough job of defining what is *ordained by God*, mainly by making their representatives (their priests) the ones who **ordain**, "I now pronounce you man and wife. What God has joined together let no man destroy."

Wait a minute! A human being **ordains**? What indicates God ordained (joined) this union? Before the man and woman said their vows - they weren't **ordained by God**? Has God complied with man's command in any other area of life? Conception? No! - Sickness? No! - Fertility? No! - Death? No! Then why would God's character submit to obeying man's command about what relationships He ordains? Acknowledging that man, even though man claims God has, does not ordain anything, is a first step, a baby step, in allowing God's messages to us to be received, consciously received.

Conversely, when one has *tuned-in* to the intricacies of feelings, one becomes aware our **God has *built into us* a natural celibacy.** All I can do is give myself as an example. In my *niave'ness*, I married at the age of nineteen. With what I knew, I believed I was making the Godly choice and was working very hard to be pleasing to God; I was a virgin until the night of my wedding. After all, any of the information from the only source I had, the church, repeated and repeated, if one followed God's laws as taught by the church, which fidelity was, one would be blessed in their marital union with another. I believed the church's *alluded to* message; appropriate sexual intimacy would follow when one *believed* (believe, choose, commit and stay true to your commitment). Oh, did I believe, I believed I was *in love* with my spouse and if I wasn't, I was going to be (this is what the non-verbal language of the Roman Catholic Church told me, and not having any more information, I believed the message), but my body was definitely going to refute and correct this belief. The denial of what my feelings were and denial of the adulterous betrayal of my husband survived totally intact, about nine to ten years, but then, truth and reality began knocking at the door of my consciousness routinely.

The body's messages, the obvious ones, that were telling me something significant was wrong during my pseudo-*in love* marriage, the *denial phase* of my life, were chronic bladder infections (no lubrication) and infertility (I had to take fertility medication to conceive both our daughters). Other than antibiotics, the treatment for bladder infections caused by intercourse (known in the medical community as *honeymoon cystitis*), is abstinence from sex; at that time, no sex was okay with me! I was so naive I only felt bad my husband couldn't have sex when he desired it. Also, my menstrual cycles were anywhere from thirty to sixty days but, after we divorced, it commenced in a normal twenty-eight to thirty day cycle. Combined with other *happenings* in those early years, I do believe my being (spirit and mind connected to body) was reinforcing that God meant me to be celibate in this relationship (despite our *ordained by man* marriage) and was trying to maintain my being in this state. (The human race does need "And may God be with you," in stead of, "And may God be with your spirit." We already have too difficult of a time consciously connecting our *own* spirit, mind and body without any more overt assistance to block our conscious aware nesses from our religious leaders.)

And now? I feel like I am married to Peter, even though on earth I'm not and even though there is no communication between us. I feel like I would be betraying *God in me,* thus, *God and me,* by trying to establish an intimate relationship with another man; I would be betraying God for what He was shown me through contact with Peter. And trying to establish a relationship with another man, definitely, would not be fair to God after God blessed me with Peter. If *falling in love* were a *choice*, I would be open to the possibility of another man in my life, but my history has already taught me that **believing** doesn't make the body cooperate, role-playing 150% doesn't work (does not produce the feelings one is mimicking), and when I wasn't expecting it at all and didn't even know IT existed, LLL showed up. I don't think I am going to *'tinker-around'* with this *state of being*; I'll only cause others and myself more pain. I've limited myself to accepting that I have no choice but to live in a state of LLL without any hope of any contact with Peter, the one who unleashes the LLL in me. Living in this mode, no contact or communication with the one I love, can't be much different than the boundaries, when one is married to someone who is comatose; if you are in *"whole being in-love"* with the comatose person there are no thoughts of looking for another relationship, an adulterous relationship. I've come to believe this is *celibacy* in *God's Law* and have accepted the boundaries.

"The body to mind messages must die." This piece of God's message is sinfully used by the Roman Catholic Church to validate an all-encompassing forced celibate life style. God's true intention is *"the body to mind messages must die"* before one's mind is free of the debris that hinders the recognition of LLL. This piece is also worthy of the phrase, "to die for the Lord," for it needs much support of achieve. Isn't it a tragic irony, when a Godly precept is followed by the church (but with an anti-God intention), for it is this that helps open the doors to/for the LLL recognition and experience, and then the church prevents what their Godly promotion helped achieve? Sadly, our society continues to be only a few growth steps away from the barriers portrayed in <u>Passage to India,</u> but I believe mankind has purchased the tickets, at least, to this passage to God's plan for His people.

Because I did not live this narrow path, either (I participated in an ordained by man marriage), the bottom line remaining for me is, there is no doubt Peter has altered my perspective of life and my energy for life, for the remainder of my life, thus affecting how I relate to those who are significant to me. Thus, the energy (or lack of) and *how I relate* has altered the lives of those connected to me, also. No man (person) is an island. And in every crowd I will continue to involuntarily look for the *face of Jesus*. I gaze into the eyes of my grandbabies and pray the children of tomorrow are spared this *bottom line*.

V
GOD'S WAY IS TRUTH, TRUTH IS GOD'S WAY

Celibacy needs to be discerned and *lived out* on the *plane of the individual*, not the *plane of the community*. No way did God mean required celibacy was to rule over any community. For man to set such boundaries at this intricately intimate level, soul level, where the recognition of LLL and vocations reside, goes against the very essence of God. For man to set such boundaries at the community level, in the way the Roman Catholic Church has done with its priests and vocations, is to make themselves a god, an idol god. If the Roman Catholic Church truly wants to be *Jesus' representative* here on earth and if they want God's people to believe, at their core level, they are, the lawmakers and loyalists must cease this idol worship.

Via Pope John Paul II, the Roman Catholic Church states, "Celibacy issues are not up for discussion." The good news is I'll be able to escape this idol worshipping monarchy; my years here have flown by and at the speed they are flying - I'll blink my eyes and I'll be gone. I'll be passing to the other side of the veil in complete confidence our God's Light and Love will be on the other side to meet me. However this is not true for the institution of the Roman Catholic Church. The church doesn't die; it is passed on from one living person, (who is a Temple of God) to the next, and any anti-God beliefs slide along for the ride, to the end of the earth, to my children and children's children. This means they will be exiled from *God's will* along with the masses. This awareness tells me, those *see* must take action or sexual dysfunction (pedophilia, rape, homosexuality, etc.), and the intolerable pain ideophrenic sexuality causes along with the pain of living, but living without life (blocked LLL union), are going to be with mankind indefinitely; in Christian religious communities who defy God, in the Roman Catholic Church, indefinitely. Rome's present perspective, their across-the-board retention of celibacy laws, aggressively enforcing those laws with more reinforcement of self control tools and only, dismissing anyone found guilty of sexual misconduct (pedophilia) from any position that has contact with children is going to insure those in-sickness do a better job of hiding their sickening misdeeds and nothing more. And, last but not least, those suffering from an ideophrenic sexual sickness will remain in the priestly ranks, if not increase, which means the children are still in danger. Please Rome; recognize the betrayal of children was intensely present before the sexual revolution of the sixties and Vatican II. Please do no return to you legalistic history. Please hear **Romans 3:20.** After all, the Apostle Paul wrote it and he is whom the Catholic Church claims to follow more than anyone.

"Now do you see it? No one can ever be made right in God's sight by doing what the law commands. For the more we know of God's laws, the clearer it becomes that we aren't obeying them; **his laws serve only to make us see that we are sinners.**"[24]

God didn't mean for Godly men to police the whole human race. People are only changed from the *inside out,* not the *outside in.* In order for people to be Godly, sometimes they must go against God's laws in order to internalize how loving God's laws are; the resulting pain convinces

---

[24] Translation from The Book,(Version of The Living Bible), Tyndale House Publishers.

us of this fact. Rome, I think you already know all this so WHY are you regressing to increased legalism?

Everywhere I turn there is evidence supporting the ultimate importance of LLL being allowed constancy. For God does have His purpose in uniting couples with LLL. For some it is beautiful children. When one considers that parents have an irrevocable effect on who their children are, and the children will probably take a higher perspective on what their parents stood for,[25] it is no wonder **God unites**, not *man* in a cleric collar. For only God knows us intimately enough to know which two people need to be united to produce off-spring with a higher perspective, a more Godly perspective.

For others, their *child* is to increase awareness that people of all nationalities and races can be seen as God's people; for others, their *child* is to break through monetary and/or social and religious boundaries. Per God, Peter and my *child* is this book, The Flying Scroll. It is denouncing forced celibacy and announcing it is NOT from God NOR pleasing to God. I believe God's original intention was to have Peter contribute his energy to clarifying the importance of LLL, also, but *free will* blocked the manifestation of His desire. Like too many *fathers*, Peter isn't present for the birth of his *"child."*

When the *marriage bed* is not **God inspired**, (no LLL present in the relationship) there isn't enough *emotional visibility*[26] in the relationship to

---

[25] From James Redfield's, The Celestine Prophecy

[26] Emotional visibility: Have you ever worked with someone who just didn't seem to understand anything you said? In talking with that person you had to explain every detail of what you are trying to say for them to get even a tiny grasp of what you meant. This would be an example of a person you had NO emotional visibility with.
Then there is that person you want to spend every lunch break with because just one word, and they know where you are coming from. Because there is no need to explain every detail for them to get-the-picture, the amount of information you can share in a given time is multiplied several times. This is an example of emotional visibility being present. Emotional Visibility is not a choice; it is the way God wired each of us. For those experiencing LLL, the emotional visibility borders on ESP (Extra Sensory Perception). Volumes are said without saying a word.

experience an emotional connection between the man and woman that is sufficient to satisfy the soul.[27] This is how I understand the "no emotional connection" between a husband and wife in which John Bradshaw, renowned psychologist, uses to explain the development of homosexuality in a son of a couple not emotionally connected. In his teachings about this path to homosexuality (there are other paths leading to homosexuality[28]), Dr. Bradshaw specifically points out, in numerous cases, the father and mother of the male child are not emotionally connected, and to compensate for this *need* not being satisfied, the mother fills this unfulfilled need, blind to her own motivation, with an inappropriate, intimate, emotional connection (and probably too much, seemingly playful, physically intimate contact during, let's say, bath or diaper changing time) with a son, when this child is still a toddler. If the parents were *in love*, **LLL**, there would be no emotional intimacy void the mother would need to fill. Combine the above with living a patriarchal lifestyle, no respect for women, and then knead in, *respect* is an essential ingredient for true intimacy, an element of LLL, the intellect does not need to work hard at all to *see* how easily one could traverse the fence from *heterosexual* to *homosexual*. All the person transferring is doing, at a core/unconscious level, is having an intimate

---

[27] Sufficient to satisfy the soul: The deepest parts of us, so deep it feels like it includes the soul and probably does, yearns, to the point of needing, for validation that our whole being (soul, mind and body) does exist. Most often we ascertain the visibility of our whole being from the reflections of ourselves we find in the responses others have to us. All humans continually search for evidence that validates their existence until the validation is found, if it is found. Religion claims to fill this need and, to a certain extent does, on the plane of the community, but it does not on the plane of the individual. God meant the LLL relationship between a man and woman to satisfy this deep need most thoroughly and in the state of marriage where LLL can do it's most productive work. (LLL will ultimately affect society with positive contributions.) This need is so strong that when a man comes from a society/family setting that does not respect women (the lack of respect for women is so deep, the thought of being intimate enough with a woman to validate the existence of self, is repulsive/nauseating/totally de-energizing.), these men are likely to transfer the fulfillment of this need onto another man, which is one of the pre-cursors to and causes of homosexuality. (Exactly what happened in Greek society in the days of the Spartans and they loved their perspective so much, they lived day and night to be the strongest, most physically perfect human male warriors to defend it, possible.)

[28] See footnote number 11 on the Spartan Civilization, page 36.

friendship and physically induced sexual feelings for the only sex they respect, the only sex they *feel* is totally pleasing to God.

As one sees and accepts that God is exposing the pain caused by **uniting** what **God** has **not united**, (the marriage was for status reasons, financial *sameness* reasons, same religion reasons, same race reasons, to escape *aloneness*, etc., etc.), a floodlight comes on! "Holi Samoli!" is this why there is so much ideophrenic intimacy in the world, especially the Roman Catholic Church and its direct descendents? Did any of you fellow Catholics grow up hearing, if you did not marry a Catholic you would be displeasing God and your chances of going to hell were much improved? How many of you had parents who prevented you from marrying outside Catholicism or had parents who were throttled by their parents from marrying outside Catholicism? Acknowledgement of the fact the religions of this world, especially Catholicism, has prevented so many from marrying for **LLL** reasons, another flood light comes on; for this means that any religion, which promotes they are the *only pleasing religion to God* upon the minds of their children, will find intimacy sins in their people. This is deduced in the Light that if Vocations are *God inspired* as the Roman Catholic Church claims, so are our *lifetime mates*. My mind cannot accept one without accepting the other. (Feelings are the indicators in both!) And until individuals can say, "I do!" to following where God leads, which may be outside of our *formative year's circle*, we just may not connect with the our Lord's intended *lifetime mate*. The more manipulative a specific religion is in keeping their young in their beliefs (i.e., a family disowns the son or daughter or one is told they will not be *saved,* if they marry someone outside their beliefs.), the more intimacy sins will be found in their ranks. These prisons with invisible, mile high concrete walls are anti-God. When and if the humans of the world stop killing each other *"in the name of God"* (war always dominates the mind as well as the headlines) for an extended period of time, there will be time and energy to see/document/ acknowledge evidence of this, this sadness in God's heart.

There aren't many, but I have met folks in the winter of their years, who still emanate signs of **LLL**. Some of these folks have been together thirty, forty or fifty-plus years. These folks frequently refer to the other as being *Jesus*, to them. Maybe these folks are trying to teach the rest of us just that! They are tangible evidence this world and its idols are not wholly successful and cannot erase LLL's survival completely. So, when and if any of you reading this know LLL has found you (there will be no doubt in your mind), you must go after it with all you have and then some. For if you don't succeed, the remainder of your life will be consumed with involuntarily *looking for the face of Jesus* where His face can't be found. If you have given LLL all the possibilities to be actualized and the powers of the world still succeed in preventing your LLL union, as God is doing with me, God will personally care for you the remainder of your life and the rest of the way *home*, in the natural celibate lifestyle.

Did your Mom, like mine, ever point out how getting cleaned-up, a bath, washing your hair, etc., on Saturday, was preparing your *"Temple of God,"* your body, for church, *"The Temple of God,"* the following morning? (Notice the capitol "T" on both "Temples!" This contradicts Roman Catholic Church practice.) When we believe the promises of God, each of us is a *"Temple of God."* In this context, it feels like an absolute oxymoron for the church hierarchy to demand a vow of celibacy for its vocations in order, at least this is their acknowledged reason, those vowed are more likely to have more time and space to work to relieve the pain of poverty, prejudice, disease, oppression, etc., in this world. Not to mention, when God has called a person to both a vocation in His Temple and a LLL union to compliment their journey, *forced celibacy* is oppression in and of itself. The causes of pain they *proclaim to the world* they are striving to relieve are no less painful or debilitating than the one (forced celibacy) they mandate to accomplish their anticipated end result (relief of pain for others). Believing forced celibacy is not destructive and is pleasing to God, parallels believing suicide, as in suicide bomber for the cause of the Muslims, is

THE FLYING SCROLL

not destructive and is pleasing to God. The *state of mind* produced by the assayers of information in each, the orthodox Roman Catholic Church and the orthodox Muslim, results in the same destruction of the *plane of the individual,* which causes the world a whole lot of overwhelming grief and anger. Oh, the anger is there! The general public just hasn't focused its eyesight enough to know who to be angry at. (Remember? a community where the *plane of the individual* has been erased is a dangerous community indeed, for they do not have any *love* for the *"self,"* therefore, cannot love others <u>outside their own support system</u>.)

In November 2003, there was a news release on a recent scientific study. According to Naomi Eisenberger, a UCLA researcher, the study compiled overwhelming evidence the pain caused by the rejection of the one you have *fallen in love* with is as painful as any major physical injury. (Many of us already knew this, right?) So why would any institution claiming to have only good and holy intentions based on *wiser than today's* (ancient) wisdom, make laws AGAINST (required celibacy for the priesthood) a union of a man and woman and portray pride in their decision? IF their source for wisdom were as wise as they contend, they wouldn't have implemented laws that were so damaging to God's people. In retrospect, because the *vowed* are required to reject the one they share LLL with, these *vowed* are actually contributing to the worlds pain; excruciating, life immobilizing and no less life altering than the injuries resulting in a person becoming a quadriplegic, pain, rather than relieving it. Would a bishop openly acknowledge that he instructed a priest, if the priest wanted to stay an active priest in the Roman Catholic Church, he had to go and punch-out the woman he discovered LLL with and keep on hitting her until she began spewing blood and fell to her knees, while agreeing never to return? Of course not! But this is precisely what is happening on the *plane of the individual,* emotional abuse. There is no way to measure the damage to the rejected. There is no measuring stick we can refer to. The ramifications are from lowered immune systems, to disease and death, to catatonic, immobilized individuals who society needs to support, to hatred of whichever sex made the rejection of LLL for idolatrous reasons (ambition, money, power, status, security, etc.). Personally, even to this day *with God's support*, twenty some years after the commencement of this condition, a daily issue I live with is I can only listen to a Christian radio station or classical music without words as the *love songs* on the general radio stations go so deep, the flood of sadness takes away the happiness of any given pleasurable moment and/or destroys my productivity in whatever I am doing. Thank you Naomi Eisenberger for supplying the evidence to formulate the language to communicate the true outcome.

    To legitimize their view of LLL and their celibacy laws, Rome has labeled the pain of not allowing accepted contact between the two experiencing LLL – as a *sacrifice, holy and pleasing to God*. God has announced just the opposite! He does NOT want this *sacrifice* and it is NOT holy and pleasing to Him. In fact, its generational consequences are all too likely to contribute to evil (in case you missed this message previously, the rejected one will likely make a vow to a non-LLL union and their offspring are in danger of living with altered sexual triggers).

    God is furious at His people for denying what they see and for not accepting what He has so frequently shown them over and over again. God wants His people to know He has no other choice but to punish His people, especially those people who are the assayers of information. God has no choice left but to punish His people for invalidating what He wants us to learn; the human race refuses to learn from its own experiences of joy and pain, for the human race cannot let-go of its human idols to admit they *understood wrong*. Mankind's, and especially the Roman Catholic Church's, obsession to have a *personal life* considered as *petty bourgeois selfishness* has got to cease if individuals are going to be able to have more energy to contribute more, more *good* to this world. [**Luke 11:52**) The *pep rallies* disguised as retreats for its priests to promote, choosing to live in LLL is *petty bourgeois selfishness* and outlining mandatory guidelines for priests to follow to destroy any such connection is appalling, anti-God, mocking God and His plan and no less damaging or less painful than cutting off the food supply of a South African nation. (The number of people damaged throughout history would fill the Continent of Africa.)

I believe Voltaire's words, "It is dangerous to be right when those in power are wrong." Just formulating the above into words makes me feel like I should install bulletproof glass in the windows of my home and car. As a quote from Jim Elliott, a renowned psychologist and author says, "There is nothing worth living for that is not worth dying for," so forward I go.

Humanities rulers want the power to *control* others with established religious belief systems, *belief systems* they silently, monetarily support. On the *plane of the COMMUNITY*, the conservative orthodox wing of any religion wants the power that erasing the *plane of the individual* gives them. On the *plane of the family*, parents want this power over their mates and children. On the *plane of the individual*, we want this power over ourselves to chose our mate or lack of a mate, to reach goals we aspire to, avoid loneliness, or simply to have children when we want them. And then there are those who <u>*want*</u> to believe their leaders, and will believe the most obvious untruth to an objective observer, so they can have someone to follow, rather than think for themselves, rather than hold themselves accountable for their actions or lack of action, rather than put out their own energy for their own brain power (which God gave them), and rather than risk *standing alone* in their beliefs. The millions, no billions of people, who have followed evil leaders from the Popes of the Inquisition to Hitler to Osama BinLaden to Hussein, ought to be enough to encourage me to take cover. But I have nothing left of value, in God's eyes, to lose, and after this book have contributed to the world all my allotment for this journey. The mind controlling influence of the idols of the Roman Catholic Church have killed any possibility that God's Will can be manifested for Peter and me, even in this land, the United States of America, which our ancestors risked their lives to reach so they and their children *could* follow God where they believed God was leading them. It appears money and powers, disguised in the package of tradition, have won.

The previous itemizes some of the consequences of believing and following the idols the earth is unwilling to relinquish and proclaims how unpopular my new aware nesses are going to be to a gross majority of the population. This is true, unless, there are more people who have recognized what's causing their pain than my mind can fathom. With all my heart, I pray the latter is true – for only then will the ones I love in this world be spared more pain because they are connected to me.

At present, the Roman Catholic Church, with its refusal to modify tradition, its huge ego ("We are the only true Temple of God"), and its royal wealth with the clout this wealth conceives and rains on its clergy, have won. There is absolutely no communication or contact between Peter and me. (It's been *Forever and a Day*.) The Roman Catholic Church is so strong, their strength, I believe, has propelled Peter into denial. "**Denial**" is a small word with huge and multiple ramifications. Books have it as their only subject and still have many of its ramifications go unmentioned. The awareness, denial is so huge it even prevents us from asking the right questions, which would lead us to a right, but conflicting place of where we *want to be*, is what keeps repeating and repeating in my mind, as the cause of God's Will being prevented, blocked and destroyed for Peter and me.

The Roman Catholic Church wants it to look to the general public like the *love* between Peter and I died of its own accord, just like they said it would, but God isn't going to tolerate this much of a victory for the church. And this is why I am *risking my life* to teach what God taught me – to anyone who can and will listen.

Peter is *revived* in my presence, but continues to give all the energy he acquires from contact with me to the church rather than *any* to a relationship with me. So I not only needed to leave to moderate the pain,

God finalized our contact and told me not to put myself in Peter's presence again. In God's Word to me (much praying and reflection, while reading the Bible), He told me what He was doing and this awareness opened doors which allowed me to follow God's command in directions I could not have risked going, when I believed there was a possibility Peter would *see* and make decisions accordingly.

In this *prescribed by God* extended *drought* (no contact with Peter), the first thing that happened was God found me another registered nurse position within the boundary of the union in which I have a career history. In my new position I would be isolated in an office compared to my previous position where I accessed the entire hospital in a given shift and would occasionally *bump* into Peter, when he visited parishioners, who were patients at the hospital.

"*Bump*" is the appropriate word for at least two occasions, for it accentuates the serendipitous nature of God's plan and deletes any possibility a human mind arranged them. One major bump was when I was escorting a patient with cardiac rhythm and breathing problems back to the Intensive Care Unit. The patient was so unstable it was necessary to transport him in the bed, as moving him to a cart could throw him into crisis; the bed, the aids who were helping me, and I took the width of the hallway so visitors were moving out of the way to allow us to get through. I was backing down the hallway beside the bed so I could keep my eye on the cardiac and the blood oxygen level monitors, when the meandering momentum of the bed pushed me into someone, who had stepped out of the way to let us through. With out lifting my eyes from the patient, I excused myself and then heard in my left ear, "anytime, anytime at all," in a low sensuous voice, a voice that was familiar and words that not just *anyone* would say in a low sensuous voice in such a moment. This conflicting information catapulted my mind into a huge conflict, do I lift my eyes from the monitors and patient to check out *who* that was? So often I wished I would run into Peter more when he was at the hospital, but didn't, so I started to erase the possibility. Whoever that was, it wouldn't be Peter, so why bother checking? But I couldn't dismiss it. The patient's vitals had remained stable so I looked up and back and to my stunned, overwhelming surprise, there was Peter in his collar, holding his prayer book, sheepishly smiling at me.

The last bump, the *bump*, arranged by God to inform Peter He was taking me away, was the day before my last day as an official member of the Flying Squad team. This time I had just delivered a patient on cardiac monitor to Renal Dialysis, which was in the Intensive Care Unit. I was backing out of the room to park the wheel chair in the hallway; Peter was walking with a family of an Intensive Care Patient and facing them in conversation. Our collision was a double shock, the shock of the collision, and then, the shock of *who* we had collided with. After he had finished with his parishioners, we had a five-minute conversation where I announced that the next day would be my last as an employee *in* the hospital. His face turned the color of gray putty and froze, and his eyes lost *life* and drooped, like his insides were screaming "Nooooo!" but only for an instant. He didn't want me to see that; he wasn't about to let me see he cared (that would be non-compliant with his advisers recommendations). So with lightning speed his professionalism conquered his soul, and he became his master again, and off he went.

VI
READY LORD, I'M READY LORD
TO FOLLOW WHERE YOU LEAD

When it is the *world* causing the pain versus *going-against-God's-Will*, God is good at neutralizing it, taking the incapacitating sadness away. During the days immediately following my acceptance that there would be *no more Peter in my life,* God could not have chosen a more positive diversion from sadness than when He blessed me with a grandchild. I am still in awe with the joy I am experiencing in the presence of my new grandbabies (I now have two)! So awesome is the joy, I have spent the last three years in transition in order to live closer to them and my daughter and her husband.

When I commenced my move, Peter was assigned to a parish close to the hospital where I am employed, but I knew it wouldn't be long before he would be reassigned, as he had been at that parish twelve years. Sure enough, two weeks before my move, when my mind was in the jogging mode to survive the transition, while maintaining a full time job, I discovered, via the diocesan newspaper, he had a new assignment. Instead of Peter choosing to move closer to me, he had chosen to move further away. The timing of this discovery feels like *God protecting me*; I believe I would have shutdown, totally, for several days if I had not been in a position where I had to keep going with something positive and pressing. I had prayed God would affect Peter in such a way he would chose to move *closer* to me, because my absence in his life would stimulate him to narrow the space between us, but if God did, Peter's free will rejected the thought. I was hoping I had heard God wrong about taking me away, but his moving in the opposite direction really made it sink in how serious God was about keeping me out of his life because of his apathetic colored choices. Still, it was an apparent act of rejection, pure and simple, and my feelings responded accordingly. If it weren't for God letting me know I was *where* I needed to be in His will, which was clothed in the delight of my grandbaby (grandbaby number two arrived in the summer of 2003), those feelings would have been incapacitating.

Through my daily chat with the Lord in the days following my move, I was informed that unless I made a connection with Peter and gave him more of the truth,[29] he would accept **LLL** had little value, and would accept the Roman Catholic Church's perspective on the condition; I was told to arrange some time with Peter. God prepared me, prior to contact that nothing would alter Peter's choices; Peter would not do anything which would threaten his role as a priest, but God wanted him to have a truer understanding of the importance, value, soul power, energy, and *Light* of the "gift" he was refusing. Realizing neither having Peter as a guest at my house for dinner nor meeting somewhere for dinner were options, it finally dawned on me, "Here I am a sinner, surely I could make an appointment with him to hear my confession." I tried to think of a sin I had committed, a sin worthy of making an appointment. Forty-eight hours after the question came the answer. Infidelity, that was it! God wanted Peter's repressed/ suppressed aware nesses to surface, and being he was the one with whom

---

[29] Not only was I to share where I was in my mind about my unchanged feelings and about how I believe God perceives our situation, Peter needed to be refreshed on the affects in himself of being in my presence, how his energy improved, devoid of any symptoms of depression. He needed to be reminded of the "*joy*."

I had committed the *perceived as sin* act, this should do it! In retrospect, I must have played a mental game with myself for there was a period of time in which I felt it was a sin I should confess. But before our appointment, when examining my conscience, I couldn't *own* that uniting with him was a sin at all, considering how God had brought him to me and vise versa, and at the time of the event, I had been told an *Army of Angels* were sent to aid in the process; *our union was what God wanted*. I was clueless as to what I could truthfully acknowledge was my reason for making the appointment, for either he wouldn't believe me or if he did, he would likely be very angry if I told him God had sent me to educate him about his choices. I *conferred* with God almost continuously about what He wanted me to communicate with Peter, but nothing fit into the framework of a *confession*. Being I had no choice, but to be truthful, the only choice open of what to confess was, *I couldn't confess I believed I had committed the sin of infidelity* (with him). Everything I did and said was pain taxingly precipitated by direction from above before our meeting, from sharing how much I talk with God, to the perspective I learned from God about my feelings for him, to God's anger at the assayers of information in the church.

The morning of what turned out to be my *(non) confession* (Saturday, October 5, 2002), arrived. The weather was conducive for traveling (God wasn't keeping me from making this appointment!), my gas tank was full and I had a container of fresh coffee for the trip. As I commenced the trip I feared four things, I wouldn't convey to Peter ALL God had directed, his response to me, mine to being in his presence for the first time in over a year, and whether I would be so overwhelmed with this fear I wouldn't be a safe driver; I prayed to God to, please, help with all four; He did. Peter's was the only car on the parking lot – so – he hadn't forgotten the appointment or worse. Upon entering the foyer, Peter appeared from the sacristy with an open smiling expression on his face. He is one who innately pays attention to detail so, when he wasn't wearing his collar; I knew he was saying he wasn't going to be judgmental (I breathed a sigh of relief). I was disappointed I couldn't be *in the moment* more, but if I allowed myself this treasure, I would probably forget God's directives so I put all my energy toward *staying focused.*

Staying focused had me choose, when offered, the Confessional over a more casual setting and the chair with it's back facing a window so I could enjoy the light shining on him versus on me. "Bless me, Father, for I have sinned...."

I had not been to confession since I was nineteen years old, and announced this as a plea for direction. Our *emotional visibility* is such that he immediately started to explain; anything I considered serious is what mattered and was appropriate to confess. Everything he did and said echoes the Theology side, not Canon Law side, of the church; so why was he so loyal to the Canon Law side? I had to make landmarks in my thoughts, over and over again to remind myself he was so I wouldn't respond otherwise. I was sad I had to concentrate so hard on what I needed to say I couldn't watch his responses.

The yellow cards I saved with an outline of what God had directed me to say that day, reveals the following:

I approached my confession in the mindset of revealing what my conscience said, but was in conflict with information presented as sinful, therefore, I needed him to give me information to correct <u>or</u> validate my conscience. The three areas I felt I could use valid moral input on were:

1.) Fornication (not adultery as my marriage had been annulled) <u>What I recall presenting:</u> "In black and white, in the laws of mankind and the church, I am guilty. But then I recall Jesus' message to the man who asked which one of the wives he would be married to heaven, 'It is not in heaven as it is here on earth.' This message always results in two thoughts popping into my mind:

　a.) of course not! – many if not all the marriages were arranged in those days, and they

　b.) were for survival and offspring, only.

THE FLYING SCROLL

Having grasped how Jesus always answered a question from the perspective of the listener, who had no way of understanding the whole/real answer, He would have minimized His answer to the level of this man's understanding. The man could only understand, 'not the same.' If the man could have understood more, I cannot, now, dismiss what the continuation of Jesus' words would be. His words would have given a message more like, 'In Heaven, ceremonies aren't needed, it's obvious which *soul lights* are together.'

Following this chain of deductive reasoning, when I listen to the readings and homilies at weddings, the passage always comes up, 'What God has joined together let no man separate,' which throws my mind into a spontaneous response. My mind *screams*, 'How can man(kind) put anything together and say God did it? How arrogant of man!' and then my mind *screams, again, 'IT'S GOT TO BE THE OTHER WAY AROUND! GOD JOINS TOGETHER AND MAN CAN ONLY CELEBRATE IT.'"*

Then Peter and I made eye contact as I continued,

Now, when the non-verbal messages I receive from you support this, HOW CAN I BELIEVE I COMMITTED A SIN?"

Pause – He understood what I meant; he understood his non-verbal actions and reactions told me he was *in*-love with me. Peter looked like he was going to say something to the extent of, "I never said.....," not,

"I don't......" In our emotional visibility, I knew he'd been over cautious not to speak a word of where his feelings were, but he wouldn't allow himself to lie, either. So, while his mind was at war about what he could say, I clarified what I had seen over the years.

"Non-verbal messages are like a dogs tail, the tail doesn't lie!" At this, it felt like he silently surrendered to the truth and sank back into his chair, which allowed him to maintain his loyalty and his honesty. Since I am not comfortable making another uncomfortable, I continued. "Peter," I said, "In good conscience with what I've learned, I just can't believe I committed the sin of fornication. Is there something I'm missing?"

Pause   –

He didn't quote church law; he didn't quote any passage from the Bible. He alluded, maybe eluded, to the only sin, probably being worthy of hell, was murder. He said it! in what seemed sincerity. He was being so kind to me (and I know he can be otherwise), I wasn't going to confront this issue. I just accepted his closure; the whole subject was too big to continue.

2.) When I divorced, I broke my vow to God (although my husband had committed adultery, which ethically alters the picture, I did "vow"). <u>What I recall presenting</u>: "Ready for the next one?"

"You have worked so hard to be true to your vows, it really concerns me that I'm not feeling more remorse for not being true to mine."

Pause – I continued.

"What seems to be preventing remorse are two issues:
- An event in my *self,* which happened during our marriage ceremony. This was no little event; it *undid* me. I actually forgot my flowers on the altar and commenced the recessional without them. What I was told was I should not have made those vows; in fact, I ended up praying, begging, God to bless us, anyway.
- Now, I feel arrogant believing, just because I made the vow – God would want it or bless it, or He'd agree with my decision. After all, us humans are puny compared to God, but how smart we think we are. So, I can't let go of, 'GOD DID NOT WANT ME TO MAKE THAT VOW. I was nineteen when I decided.

So, is my sin making the vow or breaking it? Which one hurt or disappointed God the most? I am sorry for hurting God, but I'm not sure which – hurt Him.

After being a parent, I know, like a parent, God must be very sad I made a vow which led me away from a path He may not have even shown me yet. And, from a parents perspective, God would be delighted when any human in such a spot – acknowledged the discovery that we'd made a wrong turn at the fork in the road; and took steps to back-up, find the right path, and let go of the erroneous vow (which was really against His will in the first place)."

Pause -

During the preparation for this time with Peter, I had accepted this was a lot of information and there were no pat answers to fix any of it; and unless Peter could apply what his mind had used to balance out his choices to help me understand, revise or negate the information in my conscience, there would be silence. There was silence.

(Why didn't Peter share the information he used to make and validate his choices? This was an optimum time to teach the validity of church law, at least how he saw it. This was an optimum opportunity to let me know I should know he didn't love me so my conclusions, conscience was wrong, had made and was making huge mistakes. The door to "set me straight" was so open there was even a suction trying to pull him through the open passage, and still, he wouldn't pass through it. Why?)

The possibilities of what passed through his mind, while listening and watching me struggle to stay focused, are endless. With nothing tangible to respond to, I checked my yellow card for the last directive to be addressed.

"There is one more."

3.) Pursuit of TRUTH, does it erase the sin of disloyalty to the Roman Catholic Church, when the TRUTH found conflicts drastically with church teachings and their perspective of past and current events?
What I recall presenting: "I have not been kind to the church since the child abuse issues surfaced. I have

openly accused the church of the sinful things they have done, uninhibitedly. I question myself, 'Is this sinful?' For the church has done very good things for me, also.

The church helps many people; the people in the church help many people. The church is responsible for teaching me enough about God to continue the journey. The church definitely kept me on the straight and narrow even though their straight and narrow led to a dead end; it allowed me to see and acknowledge the truth, when the truth found me. In my young adult life I had no view of the HERD of white elephants under their living room carpet.

I loved being Catholic; I loved believing I had the faith, which was most pleasing to God (this was, I believed, one thing in my life I never would need to change – my Catholicism). I loved everyone – in their humanous – being loyal to God by being loyal to their church. I had no view of even the possibility that truth could, and would collide with loyalty.

I want to find part of those secure feelings, again. I want to be sorry I have been disloyal to the church, but the thoughts get STUCK, when I try to put them in a context to be confessed. What the thoughts get STUCK in are the characteristics and ramifications of ABUSIVE BEHAVIOR. Have you studied abusive behavior?" I asked.

Pause – He shook his head, no.

"Because of Mom, I did. I wanted to understand her more so I could, hopefully, show my love for her, to her. What I discovered parallels and applies to the church!

When IN abuse, one doesn't see it; it's considered normal. A person gets used to the pain; and the pain is worth getting any amount of love from the abuser, no matter how miniscule. That speck of love is worth it! The worst part is, when the abused is a child, he/she will be an abuser as an adult, for it is the only way they know; to them it is normal. That is, unless, while they are in the pain of the abuse (during the formative years), a trusted person acknowledges to the abused that no one should hurt them like they are being hurt. The trusted person doesn't even need to physically relieve the pain of the abuse; all that is needed is acknowledgement of the fact, it is wrong. My father was this person for me. When I saw the fall out from Rome concerning their priest abusers, all the symptoms that indicated the powers in the church were the primary source of this abuse, oppressive abuse, were present. In short, the church has become the abusive parent, to me."

(I don't believe I shared the following in the manner printed here, but this is what is on the yellow cards to remind me what needed to be shared.)

"I'm still crying (inside) because I couldn't love my mother without her barring me to my bones – of energy. Now, I'm crying (inside) because I can't love the church without being stripped to the bone – of life energy.

> I ponder whether this doesn't reflect the church's money problems, too. The people love the church, but they're gasping for air. They just can't deal with another deception or be victimized by using their hard earned money for rescuing the church from its own sins. Are the parishioners angry? Yes! But, this wound is deeper than that. The ONLY way the people CAN TRUST the church, again (TRUST is NOT a choice, it is a result of what one has seen and experienced), is if the church changes their laws to give evidence of their good intentions."

Peter didn't have any information on how to place the aforesaid into a place more compatible with being an active Catholic. In his beautiful nonjudgmental way, he just acknowledged we probably should have stuck to venial sins! Being the end result of where I am is, I am sorry for being a sinner, even though I am confused about what the sins actually are, he proceeded to finalize this session of the Sacrament of Penance.

I asked if the traditional <u>Act of Contrition</u> was still used as he kindly reached past me to the windowsill to pick up a copy of, and hand me a version he likes. This version was so beautiful it actually brought tears to my eyes; I could hardly find enough control to read it.

When I had made it through the list of issues God had directed me to present to Peter, he didn't shut me out like I had feared, but neither did he share his perspective about what was said. He wouldn't expand on or attempt to correct anything; it's possible his obvious arousal was clouding his thoughts, but the lack of his self- disclosure made me feel immobilizing sadness like I had just poured my heart out, while kneeling beside his grave with no hope of any response. The one sign announcing his soul was still ALIVE was, when he tried to walk after locking the confessional door, his legs wouldn't obey him and he started to fall against the wall. He actually could not walk without hanging onto something for support. After he bounced off the wall he reached for the side of the pew to stabilize his gait. He had this bewildered, full of fear look in his eyes like he couldn't understand what was happening to him.

I saw the Angels fighting with him to believe what he was feeling, hearing and seeing; and they were in battle with his learned and accepted perspective of the above. The Angels were fighting for him to give credibility to what his feelings were showing him, and he was in battle not to hear them. I found myself in pity for him and my co-dependent prone nature surfaced; I had to help. I also had to take advantage of this moment as probably the last moment in time in which I *could* be close to him for more than ten seconds (for God told me, even this, would not alter Peter's choices), so I offered the support of my body by putting my arm around the back of his waist so he could put his arm across my shoulder for support. It took about twenty steps, through the empty church to the empty foyer, for him to gain control of his legs and *bear the weight of his being*. In retrospect, God probably wanted me to help the Angels by confronting him about his *soul* knocking his body off center for denying God's messages, but my mind flew to *pity* so fast, the Angels didn't have a chance to deliver their whole message before I interfered.

How ironic it was to discover the homily he had needed to prepare in the three hours, between my appointment with him and the evening Mass, was the very topic I had addressed with him just three hours prior; deficient monetary contributions (the only symptom the hierarchy heeds). In fact, I believe I had asked what the subject of his homily was going to be, and he declined an answer with a humorous quip. In his homily he did not acknowledge the discovery by the public of the extent of the abuse and the potential legal costs the church was paying for had anything to do with how little money was showing up in the collection plate. Maybe he couldn't guarantee their contributions wouldn't be spent for legal fees so had nowhere positive to go if he were wholly honest. His lack of portraying the complete picture of the cause of the deficient funds reeks of the church and his history of apostasy, evolutionized in this order. How can they deal with reality/truth, when they can't even say what is true?

Being I could now see even the Angels could not detour Peter's free will, when Christmas Eve arrived and my family was committed to the *other side of their family*, I was free to think and write. I emailed Peter a Christmas blessing and apologized to him for any contributions I had made to his *going against his conscience* years before. It was the only present I could think of he would want from me. Three or so days later I received his response. He apologized for any pain he had caused me, and that was it. Again there was no expansion on the subject, no denial that he loved me, no self disclosure that it was sad this is the way it had to be, nothing. I'll say it again, if at least he had told me he didn't love me, I wouldn't have to write this book (writing a book has not been my idea of what I should accomplish while on this earth!). Following this event, if I emailed him a joke or two, he would respond but not initiate any further communication. He accepted an invitation to breakfast, but after running into a parishioner and his nephew I couldn't blame him for his reluctance at the idea of sharing breakfast, again. God led me to initiate all I regretted not doing for Peter; including, sending him a dozen red roses to welcome him home from a vacation (to show Peter what he felt like when receiving caring attention from me), to show him how much I cared so he couldn't deny it to himself, and to let him know I was willing to compromise and contribute to a platonic friendship, which could allow life some of the energy, at least, to contribute to both our lives. Through all of this, God was showing him and me, *if he chose to remain active in the Roman Catholic Church priesthood,* there was *no hope for even a platonic relationship;* the *system* would not allow it, image was most important, too important. In my heart, I know we would never have been able to sustain a platonic relationship and keep our hands off each other, anyway.

As I've acknowledged before, when God really wants something he's not gentle in his messages. The last time I visited Peter at a Mass where he was celebrant (May 10, 2003), when greeting him after the service, God had me die (emotionally to *no hope*) right in front of Peter as Peter was formulating a politically correct refusal to an invitation to take some pictures of him at a future undetermined time. I had made the offer in reaction to a self-disclosure he had made, when I asked if he had a picture of himself I could have. He revealed he had only one choice, a wallet-sized portrait picture of him in his collar, which had been taken five years prior. I was sad for him as well as myself that he was declining the photo shoot as pictures of him as a person (versus a priest) must be rare, if almost non-existent. I'm sure someone in his family would be glad to have some pictures of him, and in twenty years, when all signs of prime manhood have disappeared, there would be available clear and tangible reminders of his good, non-arthritic days. (With my family and friends, I'm the one with the camera and enjoy photographing everything from family events to weddings.) From the time Peter looked away from my eyes to have space to formulate gracious words of rejection to when he eyes returned to mine, my whole state of being had changed. As he said, "I tried to email you that it wouldn't work, but..." all that repeated in my mind was, "Get me out of this gracious, politically correct, suicidal mission, and get me away from this hopeless person. God, you told me he was *hopeless*, he is!" I didn't even *hear* what came after the "but." Instantly all hope of even a platonic friendship evaporated with feelings of only being a painful thorn in his side; a thorn he was steadily prying out, solidified. In this thought, I wanted to help him get rid of his *thorn* as fast as he could, so as gracious as I could, I said, "No problem, it doesn't matter I have to go." The vision of the thorn was so clear and vivid and overpowering, I could barely formulate the, "No problem, it doesn't matter, I have to go." In this moment the change in me so shocked and confused Peter he had to turn away from the next parishioners, who were talking to him, to follow me with his eyes; follow me with he eyes out the door, again. Like always, the *real* Peter can only surface for an instant before the political Peter takes over again. His *Thinker,* as in Meyer-Briggs Personality Inventory (yes, he had shared his results with me), is so dominant; I'm sure he soon regained his power over his feelings and regained his focus on the after-service greetings.

Now that my core knows the truth; knows and believes Peter gives no value to LLL, or me in the equation which manifests LLL in him, or God as being the origin, my mind has opened up and I can *see*; all along my assignment has been and is to write this book and share what God has shared with me. I really don't have a choice but to do the best job I can. If the Roman Catholic Church is to regain the credibility they need in the eyes of their parishioners, the church must do something to prove their intentions are more pure than what they have been in the past, when they merely moved the pedophile priests from parish to parish, erased the victims from the public eye with monetary settlements (bribes), and their other deceitful pain causing choices throughout history. Allowing married clergy is the only action which will accomplish this end; because, at their cores, the parishioners know the celibate life style has *something* to do with the degree of sexual dysfunction present in the church (and we know, it is <u>only because of the legal action of the victims, not any *"trying to do the right thing,"* action from Rome, that we, the public, have been allowed this knowledge!)</u> The sagacious parishioner hears what is NOT said, like the exclusion of the cause of decreased contributions (this was before their present excuses, the war on Iraq and the declining economy), as in Peter's homily. Today's parishioner is thinking and has learned to trust his/her own deductions. Contrary to what our *own* Bishop and his faculty have released to the press, many in this archdiocese, alone, know the decreased *giving* is not wholly because of the economy.

VII
WILL I SING HALLELUJAH ?
WILL I BE ABLE TO SPEAK AT ALL ?

LLL does survive; it survives illness, crippling accidents and diseases, distance, time, in-laws, poverty, wealth, conflicting beliefs, togetherness, even a coma, etc., etc., etc. But those things, which maim it to dysfunction or non-function and does make it unrecognizable (synonym for killing it), are the same things God says are *sin, i.e., deceit, lying, adultery, jealousy, worshiping idols and so on.*

So if **LLL** is not a manifestation of God in us (the tralatitious information too much of this world believes), why then are the sins against God the same as the sins which damage and destroy **LLL?** It feels like the mass consciousness is in denial to the degree the masses have not even formulated the question. A ***Calling to a LLL relationship,*** with the *one God ordains* (is the *lifetime* mate) is **NO** different than a ***Calling to a Vocation; God inspires both.*** God is in shock that man(kind) has tried to erase the LLL calling. Man(kind) is anti-God in the extreme by mandating the *Vow of Chastity* for Vocations, for there is **nothing more chaste than an LLL union;** what can be more holy than following where God leads? What can be more evil than manipulating any person into a position of *checkmate*, where he/she must choose, but are refusing God with the choice of one of God's paths, when they choose the other God mandated path? For some are called to BOTH a vocation to lead God's people, AND to be joined with their LLL other.

Let's continue in these veridical investigative possibilities. Let's role-play that the hierarchy, the assayers of information, know **LLL** is a manifestation of God in us (we are climbing through the "Eye of the Needle"). But if they allowed this to become public knowledge, and made their laws to support the *holy union* (for example, the *holy union* deserves, **ABOVE ALL ELSE**, to be allowed the Sacrament of Marriage, including, **above** *any vowed celibate commitment)*, they believe their chauffeurs would dry up more than they already have (the world's wealthiest would discontinue their over generous contributions), their powerful *brotherhood* persona would lose its mystery, and they fear losing the power they have to control their own ranks. (Wives and families would be blamed for a younger priest not being available to be the escort of elderly priests for a vacation.)

I don't know about you, but the various pieces of the puzzle (history [including the Bible], current events, new revelations of more sexual dysfunction, more pain and abuse in the history of Christian people [commencing with and in the Roman Catholic Church] than could ever have been imagined, scientific discoveries, anthropological evidence, and last but not least, my own life experience) I have mentioned so far in the words of this manuscript fit so well together, it takes my breath away and leaves me weak. The ramification of what the Roman Catholic Church and those within her influence, throughout history to prosper in this world of idols, has done to **LLL** is so banefully huge; I can hardly write the words. The mental process I have gone through to come to these stated conclusions is the same process a Coroner goes through, when investigating the crime scene of a murder for clues to who committed the murder; combined, of course, with guidance from above. These proposed pieces of the puzzle fit so well I have no choice but to believe mankind's orthodoxy, especially in the Roman Catholic Church, has erased a path to *God being manifest in each of us here on earth,* **LLL**; my soul has felt its' worth.

Are you shaking your head in confusion? You may not be alone. Not everyone experiences LLL and if you are one who has not, yet, this will all be *Greek* to you, for there are no words to express the magnitude of the feelings present in the experience. There is no other experience in life, which causes such a *whole-being* response, to give as a reference point to help you understand. Being the non-verbal language of the world does not, even yet, tolerate much less welcome this condition, at this point I'm not sure whether I envy you or sympathize with you. In what I have heard or read about on the studies of this topic, the *phenomenon* that some have not experienced LLL is frequently mentioned. Science has documented plausible causes ranging from a genetic condition where the male is not thoroughly sexually developed, Kallmann's Syndrome,[30] to other congenital malformations, endocrine imbalance, physical (especially brain injury) and emotional injury.

When I share the following deductive possibilities (and I stress, possibilities), it is shared in a blanket of "**God made us and how we work; God made us anatomically and physiologically.**" Some see science as being on the opposite end of the spectrum from God and spirituality; they find science in direct competition with God for the souls of the world. I am not of this persuasion. I see both trying to discover how God made us and the world, where God is, and how can we be most pleasing to God in this wonderful place. I emphasize this perspective, because in some circles of religious thinking, if a *mystery* has been scientifically explained, it is no longer considered *of God's design*. These people want to see God as magical and magically overpowering the *free will* He gave each of us. This perspective, God is only active magically, "poof" and this happens or "poof" and that happens, is devaluing God's design. Several times I have heard the cliché, "*There is no one more spiritual, no one who believes more,*

---

[30] Intricately described, with its influence on priestly celibacy, in A.W. Richard Sipe's book, A Secret World, Published by Brunner/Mazel, Inc., page 216.

to their core that there is a God, than physicists." Physicists can explain everything about matter, except what holds matter together. In the fall of 2003, Nova presented a made for television *special*, which introduced recent discoveries in physics: If the numbers in the mathematical laws that answer questions at the *smaller than atom* level, the energy plane, are modified in any way, one ends up altering time, place, space, substance and, and, and! Before the narrator acknowledged the possibility, I was wondering if they didn't, in deed, discover just *where* God does His miracles! I can see a day when those who know God will need to unite with science and vice versa, to walk the last few steps to God. So far I have found the *laws of spirituality* quite similar to mathematical disciplines; when one realizes the law which dictates one set of conditions, doors open up to other astounding discoveries, when the defined law is applied to other seemingly mysterious conditions. In these beliefs I WONDER in awe about the following:

In the realm of science, doctors now have a map of the human brain, where certain thought processes are processed, and where the control centers for each part of the body is located. What totally struck me as awesome and intriguing was that the center where religious/spiritual matters are processed is directly adjacent to the center where our sexuality (feelings, desire, amorousness and behavior) is felt and controlled; they are so close they could easily and may overlap each other. The two are so close to each other, it seems quite reasonable that in some people these two areas of the brain are more intertwined with each other, allowing spiritual dimensions to enter the realm of sexuality and vise-versa, than others. Now I have combined this piece of science and the documented history of romantic love with spirituality, resulting in a neoteric awareness of some other possibilities.

When I discovered what God has indicated as sin parallels and probably is the same as that which destroys LLL, it dawned on me that those who have NOT experienced LLL quite possibly have not been able to **let-go and let-God** in their daily lives. Rephrased, it is quite possible those who have not had LLL descend upon them have made choices for ego reasons/*status in the community* reasons or simply, security reasons, etc. – rather than/versus – "*being-ONE-with-God*" reasons in too many areas of their lives. With an evolutionary *(like)* process in mind, I wonder whether the more we individually attempt to be *good* like Jesus, if those two sections of the brain don't overlap each other more. This last possibility does deserve a book of explanation, but stick with me, with this thought in mind before invalidating the possibility totally. (If sufficient funds were available, an investigation would be very interesting.) And please understand, while assessing the following, since my discovery that what I used to understand only as a metaphor depicting mental events are, in reality, tangible happenings (i.e. *thunder*), the following probably feels more plausible to me than to someone who has not had the experience of LLL, to undo some of the erroneous preconceived ideas of the true meaning attached to different words in our language.

If *good*, pleasing to God choices do cause a physical change in our being and one of those changes is opening the pathways between the spiritual and sexual portions of the brain, this physical change could be recorded on the human chromosome, and be passed down to future generations. This feels like a very plausible explanation for why, throughout history, *romantic love* has taken a path, which compares to a type of evolution[31] down through the generations of civilized man. In the days of Jesus, man and woman did not marry for *love*; they married for economic reasons, child bearing and rearing to ensure their survival (for young men to fight their wars), raising crops, hunting and so forth. Everything was for the community and nothing for the individual. In psychology this view of the male/female relationship is termed "Tribal Mentality." (The megalomaniacs of this world still want all of humanity

---

[31] Intricately documented in Nathaniel Brandon's book, The Psychology of Romantic Love, pg 11-13, Bantam Books

in this mode.) It's no wonder Jesus gave the message that marriage, as they knew it, did not exist in heaven. Then the teachings of Jesus started affecting the lives of those following Christianity, where the individual is pronounced to have great importance; God will search high and low to find the ONE *sheep* that is lost; God knows the thoughts of each and everyone of one us; God knows every hair on our head and every sparrow that falls. These statements do make each of us individually important. What Jesus taught gave permission/allowed humans to accept, *we as individuals are important*. Before Jesus, an individual could not accept that he/she had any personal value; the whole concept was foreign to the human mind. In Jesus' time, this perspective was a whole new revelation. Jesus lives to be an example of what is *good;* and his followers, us, attempt to emulate him and as we do so, we become more *good*.

Having accepted what Jesus called *sin against God* and those actions/beliefs, which damage and destroy LLL, are coequal; it makes perfect sense to me that the more a person has emulated Jesus and the more a person has achieved what Jesus was teaching, the greater the probability is, he/she will experience LLL, also. Just *wanting to do good* and living to the best of ones ability to do so, surely would lead one closer to, if not down, a path where LLL could be seen, experienced, acknowledged and actualized, which would indicate Christianity isn't the only arena where LLL can be found; all, genuinely seeking truth and goodness, thus God, have developed pathways which can/will allow LLL to be experienced.

The most tangible, probable and frequent explanation of why some do not experience LLL is a life altering, traumatic psychological event(s), which happened in their formative years (child abuse, death of parents/ immediate family member (especially if violent), a serious illness in the family, incest, etc.). This *traumatic to the nervous system event(s),* delayed or halted their emotional maturation by scaring the pathways of the brain, scarring which also included the pathways between the *spiritual* and *sexual* areas, interrupting the communication between the two. (Newly documented findings disclose, especially during the toddler years, when our brains are still in the process of being wired, alterations can and are made.) LLL is both, spiritual and sexual, requiring interaction between the two portions of the brain.

The list of possibilities goes on and on. From people, who, through no fault of their own, are unable to own the *state of being* (the above mentioned possibilities plus accident, illness, or war, may have prematurely taken the intended LLL's life, the *two* shall never meet), to people, who have the mental/physical capability, but are intensely employed in activities for achievement, survival, *people pleasing,* and/or maintenance of life with no time to *think,* or meditate, or pray will have road blocks to the *state of being,* and/or, road blocks to even recognizing their LLL connection. Like the road to Heaven, the road to LLL is narrow and winding.

If those of you, who have not experienced this phenomenonal *state of being,* would role-play for a moment that you can see LLL is part of God's plan for His people; in this mode, could you, would you *see* the possibility of the following deduction?
If you, anyone could empathized with God for losing His precious souls to such a deviation from the truth about the importance of LLL, can/could you understand why God has allowed today's calamity of the child sex abuse cases damage, "*bring to its knees,*" the Roman Catholic Church, a major contributor to distorting God's plan for His people throughout the ages?

When fitting the pieces of this intricate mosaic puzzle together, one cannot ignore where Christianities roots lie, in Judaism. The <u>Tribal Mentality</u> definition for marriage continues to reside within Judaism's traditions, and the idols of the world, including money and power, have oppressed LLL in their societies to this day. On my knees, I wonder if this wasn't an aspect of Judaism Jesus was challenging. We'll never know for sure, as too many of the original writings have disappeared. But there is nothing in what we do have access to that contradicts this observation. Also, when reading the Book of Job, have you ever been aware of a huge chunk of missing information, which is so huge it insults the mind that it isn't there? We are taken through the possible causes of Job's suffering in intricate detail and then it drops off a cliff. There is nothing until he is an old man, married, and with several children. Even before LLL descended on me, I was aware of this huge chunk of missing information and my mind wondered if something about *"falling in love"* hadn't been extracted. Since LLL has descended on me and in combination with how the Book of Job ends, by increasing the value of woman by including his daughters in his will, being married and having many children, I am very convinced of the possibility/probability the missing chunk of information would have helped clarify the importance of LLL for mankind. What is the conclusion that brings me to this end? Job had fallen in love, but didn't want it. All his body's illnesses were because he was refusing to follow God into a LLL relationship. When he finally relented to God's will and united with his LLL other, his body healed. This is the only explanation his story ends the way it does, emphasizing what was emphasized. I yearn to read the missing chunk!

When Christianity evolved from the Jewish faith, devalued LLL came along for the ride; only the Roman Catholic Church added more devaluating non-verbal messages. Stories are a powerful teaching tool and the *powers in control* are immensely aware of it. Watch any fictional story made for the big screen or television and if the writer and/or producer are supporters of either Judaism or Catholicism, just watch; their messages will attempt to eradicate any importance given to LLL. I have come to anticipate the outcome of the story by who wrote the material, book and script.

I believe God wants, with all His essence to have all the people of the Roman Catholic Church enter the *Promised Land* (actually, all *truth* seeking individuals), but the Roman Catholic Church's denial of the very essence of God and its ideophrenic sexual ramifications have made God so angry, He has sworn the Roman Catholic Church, as a unit, would never enter the *Promised Land*, the place of rest He had planned for them. **[Psalm 95:11]**

VIII
WE HAVE BEEN TOLD, WE'VE SEEN HIS FACE

He knows every Hair on our head and every thought, which crosses our mind; shouldn't we care enough to do the same? Because it's on the *plane of the individual* where sins originate, we need to become acutely aware of how to identify sin at our core level, for the sins of individuals accumulate – leading to the sins (which are then accepted as a *way of life*, normal*)* of whole communities. Since the larger picture has come into focus, it feels like the community of the Roman Catholic Church is among the founding fathers of, rather than, an exception to this process. The anti God celibacy laws are causing their own to NOT accept God's individual plan for each of them, which separates a person from living out *who* and how God made them. For example, in his core Peter knows he loves me in the LLL sense; he knows the energy flowing between us is life giving, yet he cannot or refuses to acknowledge it outwardly, at the *thinking, conscious,* level. He cannot *be* who God made him to be, openly. God does not want us to need to do this to ourselves to survive. We cannot be ONE with God, when we need to compartmentalize our feelings and experiences to survive. God does not want us to simultaneously put one of His callings/ feelings/experiences (the Sacrament of Ordination) in an "acceptable compartment" of our brain, while putting another of His callings/feelings/

experiences (to connect with one's LLL other for the Sacrament of Marriage) in an "unacceptable compartment." (In the extreme, people with split personalities or multiple personality disorders do this.) Or Jesus would not have emphasized the importance of ONE; our *person* needs to be ONE, not many. On the *plane of the individual,* the words of Jesus, as translated in The New American Bible, says this best:

Matthew 16:24-26

Jesus then said to his disciples: "If a man wishes to come after me, he must deny his very self, take up his cross, and begin to follow in my footsteps. **(25)** Whoever would save his life will lose it, but whoever loses his life for my sake will find it. **(26) What profit would a man show if he were to gain the whole world and destroy himself in the process? What can a man offer in exchange for his very self?**

On the *plane of the individual,* denying the *"very self,"* means you don't follow your knee-jerk response to be physically safe or protect your image by saying 'Yes," when you mean "No," or vise versa, to be pleasing to people or to stay out of trouble or to be politically correct, etc. Any deviation from *truth, reality and* good the conscious mind takes – a chunk of the *soul self* dies. As is also relevant to the LLL issue, feelings are the indicator in recognizing a call to a vocation. For a vocation, feelings are so valid they are considered a *sign,* but for marriage, feelings are alluded to as invalid, as far as criteria for the choice of a mate is concerned (the word *feelings* isn't even mentioned). How can ONE institution perpetrate TWO values on one word, feelings? In other words, compartmentalize *the value of feelings* into an "acceptable compartment" for one situation, and simultaneously compartmentalize *the value of feelings* into an "unacceptable compartment" (of the brain, thought process) for a different situation?

"*Take up his cross*" would mean being open to whatever/where ever your core TRUTH leads you (what you hear your internal voice saying), you are willing to go, abandoning ambition, reputation, etc. (Again, this includes ones life time mate as well as vocations.) Not an easy thing to do. (This is how I understand *"Let Go and Let God".)* At this core level of thought, follow the aforementioned verse through to the end. There is NOTHING a man can offer "in exchange for his very self." You have *free will,* you can alter your "very self," the "self," who hears God's messages, can be destroyed; is no more. Those who are doggedly attempting to be what others want them to be instead of who and how God made them will not be ONE with God, the "self" is no more. There is no profit in this whole world worth "destroying the self" for.

The closest Peter came to his outside and inside being ONE was when he gave me the gift of the Galway Irish Crystal heart jewelry box with the Claddagh emblem embossed on the top.[32] At the time of this precious gift I had not heard the tale associated with the Claddagh ring. Not until the next morning did I read the pamphlet accompanying the beautiful crystal heart with the foreign emblem embossed on its cover. I sat for hours stunned and confused. Finally I had to pick up the telephone and dial his number to inquire if he was aware of the meaning of the emblem for I didn't want to believe something, which wasn't meant for me to believe. Upon the inquiry there was silence, then a distant voice saying, "Yes," and nothing more. He had opened a door, but I had no clue what to do with this milestone event or if I should believe what I wanted to believe. Maybe he already regretted giving me the gift! (Had Peter's *"self,"* already, retreated, and now, the *political Peter* was in control?) Months later, when I couldn't stand my confusion anymore, I asked him to describe his feelings for me. All the *political Peter* would own is, it is *physical attraction,* a politically correct description in his world, our world; a description which allows it to be believed that it is something which should be controlled, mastered and diminished into *nothingness* in order to be pleasing to God

---

[32] See 'the history of the Claddagh symbol, footnote number 15, page 39.

or as many of those in the general public see it, for the future safety and well being of their children and for the good of the community. (*Letting go* and *letting God* is scary; and being it is necessary to actualize LLL, LLL feels dangerous, also.) It cannot be denied, Peter's apparent perspective is a mirror reflection of what Rome and her conservative loyalists perpetrate as God's perspective.

It has not been easy for Peter to follow the conservative orthodox Roman Catholic path. During the days in which we Catholics were still feeling the liberating vibrations from the reign of Pope John the Twenty-Third, he was at least faithful to me as a person. Since the *injured loyalists* in the Church have organized their strength to prevent any further disgrace, the Church hierarchy has put a strangulating neck lock on its priests to portray to the public a sterling image; Peter wouldn't even take a chance of going against their guidelines to write me a note of consolation when my parents died, or simply telephone me with a consolation message. He knew I was the only one my parents had to take care of them; he knew I was *in* their deaths alone. The one living sibling I have is male, he lives too far away to be part of their death process and his wife was *there* for him so he didn't need me to share in our grief. God has spent a lot of time *carrying me*, without anyone to help lighten His load.

Here however, I must rescue Peter's character (a compliment is overdue), the part of himself he used to reveal more often. In the summer of 1999, my father was already gone and my mother was entering her last chapter, the last few pages of her last chapter. Anyone close to her knew the challenge of being in her presence, from the couple friends she and Dad had in their early retirement years to the nursing staff, who cared for Mom during the last days of her illness, there were many who apologized to me for not spending more time with Mom, or empathized with me and wondered how I could continue caring for her. It had become apparent

THE FLYING SCROLL

Mom could no longer live independently and she was bulldozing me into taking her into my home; she wasn't going to accept any other decision.

Since I believe it was her angry, unhappy attitude and verbal/emotional abuse which commenced the scenario of events which led to my father's death (her perspective of every situation and her behavior literally destroyed his will to live), I knew there was no way I could have a constant diet of her, a twenty-four hour a day diet, and survive emotionally intact. I investigated independent living facilities, found a Catholic community, which was beautiful and she could afford, but I needed her approval to go forward and reserve a unit for her. Knowing the only human beings Mom will put forth the effort to produce charitable thoughts for were priest's, I telephoned Peter and through tears of frustration (probably mixed in with tears of a broken heart) presented the situation and asked if he would talk to her. At first Peter thought I was asking him to come to my home to talk with her so he declined. (See! Those retreats in Sioux Falls, South Dakota, work!) When he discovered in conversation that she was in the hospital, he agreed to visit her after his last service the following Sunday morning. Mom did *put her better foot forward,* as anticipated, and stated the assisted living apartment was a good idea. In overflowing thanks to Peter I could proceed preparing a place for Mom to live, even though she continued to mumble about not understanding why she couldn't live with me.

Mom never made it to her new home. The following week the inoperable blood clot sitting in her aorta, which had been intermittently blocking the flow of blood to her small intestines, permanently lodged in the Ciliac artery and destroyed her bowel. Within hours she proceeded to sink into septic shock. When I became aware that we had only hours before she would be gone from us forever, I had to follow through with what I believed would be her last request if she could communicate one; I had to give her the opportunity to have the Sacrament of the Sick, so again I called Peter and he came right over. I told Peter I would be surprised if Mom lived till morning; it felt like he did NOT believed me. (This wasn't the first time I had shared some information, which he didn't believe, but proved true. When the reflex action is to NOT BELIEVE a female, the Non-verbal Message number II, on page 124, is too likely a major cause.)

After he had blessed Mom, I accompanied him to the elevator. He asked why I had called him instead of the priest the hospital had on-call (here, Mom was dying, she was semi-comatose, and this was his choice of words?). I told him it was because if he came, two blessings would happen instead of one; Mom would be blessed for her transition from this world to the next, and I would be blessed with energy to make more wise decisions and be with her all night, energized, so she would know she was not alone for a second. Thanks to Peter, there was not one more thing I could think of I could do to satisfy what I believed would be Mom's last wishes, and **thanks to Peter** (despite his focus), I had the energy to hold and comfort Mom through the night, notify my brother that if he wanted to see her he needed to come, now, and make all the arrangements which need to made at death's door, without falling apart myself.

Peter didn't allow me his reaction to the knowledge I needed him. The morning after Mom received the Sacrament of the Sick, the morning of her death, September 27, 1999, was the last communication I had with Peter until my (non) confession in 2002, two years later. Taking shallow, short breaths to keep myself away from tears, just before 7 a.m. I went to the nurse's conference room to use the telephone to notify him that Mom had taken her last breath about 6 a.m. He sounded stunned. "Pat, I'm so sorry!" came his stifled, struggling to be professional, exclamation through the receiver. I responded by *matter of factly* thanking him and reinforced his coming, of course, had helped Mom, but also had helped me, which helped me help Mom.

Especially after his involvement in Mom's passing, knowing Mom and Dad during their retirement years, knowing my daughters since they were in grade school, and being acquainted with my brother; it feels completely unnatural Peter never sent a sympathy card or never telephoned to inquire if my oldest daughter was able to fly home from Warsaw, Poland, to be with the family (she did). He absolutely would not acknowledge having a special place in his heart for me, verbally or non-verbally. He wanted to be sure I believed I was no different to him than any other US citizen. I did not even receive the caring a parishioner of his would receive. I often wonder how Peter feels, when he forces himself not to do what his *core self* instructs, or does what his *core self,* his feelings, vehemently object to. Does he lock the *fallout* inside as part of his job? Does he contact a support person? Maybe he is instructed to contact an assigned support person, who helps enable him to live with the pain of causing pain (a temporary fix). Did Peter's realization of what I was going through cause such overwhelming feelings of guilt for the aloneness of my situation he couldn't communicate one word for fear of what other words would involuntarily leave his mouth? Couldn't he write a note without saying, "If you need to talk, just let me know?" Because he had done this once before, we ended up seeing each other one on one. He even acknowledged he should not have written that note on a Christmas card; because it did commence contact with each other. I'll never know. Something happened to shut down his character. What could cause one to repress or suppress a natural caring reaction in a situation like this to this degree?

    I have deduced two probabilities. I do believe he sought out *loyal-to-the-vow-of-celibacy* counseling, probably priest to priest, probably in Sioux Falls, SD, who taught him the picture he needed to paint to be successful at interrupting the momentum of his feelings, thus the future of our relationship. He did succeed in interrupting the future of our relationship, but as indicated earlier, his feelings continued to affect his desires and decisions about what to say "yes" or "no" to, and his feelings literally knocked him off balance so he had to struggle to walk. The other probability is that he attends those *pep-fests* to support the perceived value of, and reinforce how to maintain the celibate life-style. The main purpose of these retreats is to convince the attendees the celibate life style is the **most pleasing** lifestyle to God. This perspective is promoted by utilizing the *brotherhood* as an individual's emotional support versus a *significant other* in the *outside* world (which is equivalent to the words in the Bible, "heathen wife") and only allows each celibate the information the community wants them to hear about intimate relationships, helping to insure their loyalty. Therefore *individual* messages from God, which have any signs of romantic love, have no value, are erased, discredited, mocked, ignored, and downright murdered. If the non-verbal messages of these priests (complying with forced celibacy says they believe the celibate life style is more pleasing to God than the married life style, no matter what, or they would not have allowed themselves to vow to celibacy) don't erase the verbal messages from the pulpit (they believe God sees the married lifestyle as equally pleasing to God), the non-verbal message surely speaks louder than the verbal. Remember, everyone has a more tangible, conscious ability to agree or disagree with verbal or written messages; conversely, our core *realizes* the non-verbal message, most often without an awareness of the moment the message was received, and a person does not have the opportunity to agree or disagree. The non-verbal communication of the anti-individual perspective found in the *celibate lifestyle* not only defines celibacy as more pleasing to God than marriage, but also turns LLL into evil's tool in their minds, and the minds of anyone who is watching with an open vulnerable heart. (Why isn't there more anger expressed by married Catholics at this non-verbal message? Are we so accustomed to accepting inconsistencies, oxymorons, that our thoughts don't even trip on these lies?)

On the *plane of the individual*, when a person says one thing and does the opposite, what do you believe, what they say or what they do?

God is the *Master Manipulator* of earth; we call the results from His manipulation, natural consequences. The horrendously tedious manipulations orchestrated by the church say the consequences <u>they have formulated</u>, they want us, the public/parishioner, to believe God did. Now, if that's not crowning oneself God, I don't know what is. Since God gave us *free will*, allowing mankind to choose to manipulate each other and our environment in His name, those wanting to remain in power or gain power have chosen to utilize this tool, albeit with deceit and lies.

On the *plane of the community*, the more life experience I tuck under my belt the more exceptions to, *"when there is a choice, it is wiser to believe what one sees before believing what one hears,"* I discern. The lack of language to formulate a mental picture of all, and/or what is communicated with non-verbal messages complicates communication on the subject even when the mind is more cognizant of the existence of the non-verbal messages. This is precisely *why* the whole human race hasn't been able to protect itself from negative, deceitful, non-verbal messages. So please bare with me as I attempt to put into words this convoluted system of communication. What I have sensed leads me to the awareness, many in power have taken the truth, *"what is seen and/or experienced is believed more than what is said,"* and used it against reality by deceitfully manipulating consequences. Without language to protect the *self*, the *individual* internalizes, without question, the message at the subconscious level. At the subconscious level, a person isn't immediately aware any message(s) has even been accepted, but a whole new list of preferences and rules will affect the way a person *plays out* each moment of existence. Conversely, for example, when a person discovers a preference has changed (i.e. he used to enjoy this or that, but now doesn't, or he/she is feeling guilty about something, which shouldn't cause guilt feelings and in the past, wasn't an irritant), this person is unable to consciously recall the event when the non-verbal message, which altered their being, was delivered. A master manipulator knows this truth to his/her core and intuitively uses this power in every aspect of his/her life over those in his/her life, whenever he/she sees/feels that doing so would advantage *their* world, their beliefs and/or their support system. A non-verbal message may be as simple as not laughing at a good clean joke, when a person with a conflicting belief tells it, to being fired from your job, because you told the truth about your company and the truth was not pretty. Such a non-verbal message was given to all who knew the former diocesan editor,

John Strange, who was fired by Bishop Joseph Gossman for printing what another person said; "The Catholic church is broken and wounded and in need of some healing."[33] What the non-verbal message, the involuntary dismissal from his job, said to all who knew about the circumstances was, "Unless you want more trouble than you are willing to have, you had better not openly acknowledge the truth about the present condition/popularity/ credibility of the Roman Catholic Church." An example was made of John Strange. Master manipulators are intelligent people and know when a situation is *gray* (no language to clearly identify the true message so it can be overtly, consciously contradicted) enough to work. Most master manipulators are *super sensitive* enough to avoid an extreme, obvious, overt situations, such as the one just described, for they instinctively know what is workable when. The person manipulating knows, if the power (the non-verbal language) leading the way cannot be challenged verbally, he/ she has won. All too often they knowingly use this knowledge to gain power over people, while convincing themselves it is a non-sinful activity. (Some in the business world pay instructors to teach their mangers the tools to implement it.) Those in power, who are delivering the *anti-God, non-verbal directions* to manipulate mankind, want those being affected/manipulated to believe their intention(s) is *good* – so they adamantly claim any other message delivered is an accident. When the *powers* do not change what is giving the *anti-God, non-verbal message,* the words coming out of their mouths are only rubbish, words they know **you** need and want to hear and they must say to be credible (usually supported by a popular, accepted belief), but their words are **not** their true intention. They also know their non-verbal message will negate or impair the outcome of their words, which is their desire. Yes, there are some circumstances in life where an action made with a *good intention* does cause the wrong non-verbal message(s), but when realized, the non-verbal message is corrected also.

---

[33] National Catholic Reporter, January 9, 2004, Patrick O'Neill is a freelance writer living in Raleigh, N.C.

When ANY power says one thing but makes it mandatory to live out the opposite, *one can bet* the words the people accepted in their minds as truth, (what a person has heard from God), are from God, are what God wants for His people. But the power, who is saying those words, doesn't believe the words their lips are forming, and are simply using *godly* words; words they know the person they want the loyalty of wants to hear, and will accept. The master manipulator has another motive in mind than the words he is saying indicate, for he/she is simply using their carefully chosen words to make your mind vulnerable to the acceptance of something you would not accept if you had the choice. The master manipulator's real messages, which are in conflict with truth and God's desire or they would be verbally stated, are present IN their non-verbal language, where the listener is more vulnerable, will absorb the message at a deeper level, and have few if **no** tools to rebuke or negate the message in their own minds.

God made our brains so awesome - all these tediously listed inter-relational events happen almost simultaneously on the plane of the individual, one person to another person. On the plane of the community the opposite is true. *Mega* amounts of time are spent initiating, organizing and refining non-verbal events to give the subordinates their messages, leading to beliefs the *powers* want the subordinates to have. There are centuries of refinement in the strategies we see today. Too many *in power* want to keep their power no matter how anti God their tools are, especially, as it turns out, too many of our pretentiously pious religious leaders.

IX
ON EAGLE'S WINGS

The Roman Catholic Church will not acknowledge they give the following messages in any way, shape, or form. Most likely they will reiterate their proposed rationalizations for *why* it is *the way it is,* and apologize for any misunderstandings. Oh, there is no doubt many of the leaders genuinely believe there are legitimate reasons for the laws and circumstances that scream these non-verbal messages. Some of the churches leaders will try to counterbalance these non-verbal messages with lengthy articles emphasizing the importance of marriage and what a blessing from God it is; some Bishops[34] have already gone this route. This written message is to appease the *thinking* reader for they know the non-verbal message will accomplish the end result they desire despite their words. But, when God Speaks, the words and the non-verbal message(s) are ONE; they support each other versus contradict each other. In fact, this is the major element we can consciously use to critique what our

---

[34] In the January eighth and fifteenth 2004 editions of the St. Paul and Minneapolis Diocese newspaper, The Catholic Spirit, Bishop Harry Flynn 's weekly commentary is entitled, "Between Man and Woman: Questions and Answers About Marriage and Same-Sex Unions," is where he does just this; he put heterosexual marriage on a pedestal in church eyes. Heterosexual marriage belongs on this pedestal but at an even higher level, above mandatory celibacy for it's vocations (oppressing LLL by keeping it less important than vocations literally erased the proclaimed message), where making their words and non-verbal messages ONE, will put it.

inner self absorbs, "Are they ONE?" If we are to be pleasing to God, this aspect of the equation cannot be denied, but I'm sure some will try.

EXAMPLES OF WHAT THE NON-VERBAL (SUBLIMINAL) MESSAGES OF THE ROMAN CATHOLIC CHURCH TEACHES:

(This section is more a summary of already stated issues so you will find some redundancy as well as new material. The repeated information is needed to give a more complete picture of how each of these non-verbal messages affect and influence our beliefs, thoughts and behaviors.)

I.) FORCED CELIBACY FOR ITS VOCATIONS:

TEACHES **no sex** is MORE PLEASING TO GOD than a life in a committed interpersonal heterosexual lifetime relationship, *especially, when a marriage has erotic sex.* (How ironic this message is from an institution that thought nothing of castrating male boys to keep their voices from lowering.) There is no written history of a community with celibate religious leaders in Jesus' time; the thought of such a possibility was likely very foreign. I'll wager that if this thought were presented to Jesus, he would have been wide eyed in stunned silence. Many of mankind's inventions have been shocking to God, thus would have been shocking to Jesus. From this perspective, viewing the passage *"Blessed is the man who voluntarily restrains from sex for the Kingdom of God"* to mean he wanted communities of celibates serving God is a baneful joke. One needs to know that at the time this was written marriage was overtly promoted to bear children to increase the number of members in their society. A celibate brotherhood would have been voraciously frowned upon for not contributing children. So how could the interpretation of the church be correct? Also, on the *plane of the individual* where actualization of a LLL union is a primary element of the "Kingdom of God," the message of these words is more likely to mean, "Blessed is the man who does not marry because he is more pleasing to God being celibate outside a LLL relationship (versus marrying a non-LLL spouse)." Or the man, being referred to, was prevented from joining his LLL other so chose a single life, which would not contribute children to the society, and this man needed the support of this message from a credible source in society to be an accepted member of the society he lived in.

Let's combine all the information in the Bible the church uses to support their mandated celibacy laws into one coin – and flip the coin – all this biblical information, from individual verses to whole lifestyles (including the Apostle Paul's), can be seen as validating the importance of a LLL union, and its natural celibacy desires outside of this union, which God wants us to obey.

Have you heard of any communities of celibates in Jesus' world? When none existed, Jesus wouldn't even have cause to reference such a condition as *a whole community of celibates.* And if Jesus was fond of the idea, wouldn't he have taken this opportunity, when he supported *"the man who restrains from sex...,"* to announce it? Being the Roman Catholic Church has taken such privileges with Jesus' and the Apostle's messages, let's apply these privileges (as the Roman Catholic Church will claim I am doing with the following) to

1 Timothy 4:1-6.
"But the Holy Spirit tells us clearly that in the last times some in the church will turn away from Christ and become eager followers of teachers with devil-inspired ideas. These teachers will tell lies with straight faces and do it so often that their consciences won't even bother them.

They will say it is wrong to be married and wrong to eat meat, even though God gave these things to well-taught Christians to enjoy and be thankful for. For everything God made is good, and we may eat it gladly if we are thankful for it, and if we ask God to bless it, for it is made good by the Word of God and prayer."[35]

Now, what Christian community has ideas that parallel the "devil-inspired ideas" of "wrong to be married" (forced celibacy for the priesthood is just this), and "wrong to eat meat?" (Is it Friday, anyone?) And, "tells lies with straight faces?" (A clue: Before evidence proved otherwise they said, "I don't remember, when we'd received a report(s) about a particular priest having inappropriate sex with a child, whether we just moved this priest to another parish.") Your mind didn't need to work too hard for the answer, did it?

II.) NO FEMALE PRIESTS:

TEACHES God does not respect woman as much as men and does not want women representing God/Jesus in this world. As stated in Chapter IV, THIS IS THE AIR I BREATHE,[36] this is no small, insignificant, message. Many a man wants to absorb and has absorbed this message, whether they consciously admit it to themselves and/or the world or not. Who would want to be "ONE" with a perceived "*unworthy to represent Jesus in the world*" person? I wouldn't! Role playing that I believe this message, gives me the feeling that it wouldn't be much different intimately communicating with a *monkey* than it would be intimately communicating with a woman. If and when a male does involuntarily absorb this message,

---

[35] Translation from The Book,(a version of The Living Bible) Tyndale House Publishers
[36] Found on pages 62-63.

it is no wonder their *knee jerk reaction* is to invalidate what any woman says. They likely even WANT to value what a woman says, but this absorbed message prevents it from happening. Thus, in reality, this non-verbal message has caused many a marriage to fail!

The whole conspiracy against LLL parallels the conspiracy to keep me in denial about my own body, the cause of the STD (sexually transmitted disease). The civilian doctor at the Wiesbaden Air Force Hospital (Germany), a kindly Turkish grandfather type, would take my husband aside for private conversations. This doctor knew something was going on in my mind that kept my body from appropriately responding to sex. I was very irritated that I was excluded from these conversations, which were obviously about me (it felt like my parents were deciding my future), but if there was any hope of preventing more bladder infections, almost anything was worth it, including being irritated. Being "VD" (venereal disease) was stamped on my Dependent Military Medical Record, this Turkish Urologist knew our history and this was what their conversations were about. I had clung to the idea that they were discussing the necessity of adequate foreplay before intercourse, when the reality of the situation was the physician believed I had shut down secondary to my, then, husbands adultery. (I was always curious why this Turkish physician was so overly patronizingly kind to me!)

Why wouldn't they discuss this with me? The surface piece is the physician and my, then, husband believed I would leave and divorce him if I consciously knew about the adultery, and they were likely correct. TRUTH is a mighty sword, a mighty sword I respect, and I also understand humans make mistakes so the outcome is really unknown. BUT the insidious *beneath the surface* piece of "why" I was not allowed the truth was because the military is a *"Brotherhood"* just like the priesthood, neither the physician nor my, then, husband saw any evil in stealing a choice from a female about her own destiny. Neither the physician or my, then, husband believes a female deserves TRUTH, which brings us the long way back to God. This belief is also the residual of viewing women as *"not worthy of being God's representative on this earth"* message passed down through the generations. This message produces an, "it is GOOD to deceive a female, when it keeps her *"in line,"* message. Was it "GOOD to keep a black slave illiterate to keep him or her *"in line"?* This needs to be perceived as the same issue, but it isn't.

God is Truth. If Truth were allowed to take the lead, yes, there probably would have been a divorce about 1969, but the divorce would not have injured two innocent children; they were not born until 1973 and 1979.

And men aren't the only ones that have absorbed this, "women are not worthy of be God's representative on this earth" message; females see, more accurately, feel themselves in this light, also, and feel men are more worthy. Our children are female and to this day have more loyalty to their father than their mother (me), with the knowledge of his adultery and the probable ramifications. But like me, his denial allows their mind an open door to some other magical possibility, because they don't *want* to believe it. My soul cries with this message for mankind; Truth hasn't the power to rise above generations of believing, at our female core, that we even deserve TRUTH. The oldest daughter has taken some huge growth steps in this arena, though. Something in her realizes where the error(s) have been made so she is searching. She wants to be a pastor and has been accepted at Yale University's School of Theology (even though she is an active Catholic). But her five years as a school counselor at an American school in Warsaw, Poland, has left her in need of time to re-energize, and time to evaluate whether going to Yale is financially feasible. (The Roman Catholic Church has lost another *gem* to the Protestants!)

III.) No Dispensations From Rome:

TEACHES the Church is God! *TEACHES* that God is not present IN our growing and maturing thoughts and feelings; and *TEACHES that* making mistakes is unforgivable. **What an un-Godly thing to do to Godly men.**

IV.) When There Is Any Communication About Sinful Sex, "Every Union Outside The Marital Union," Is Portrayed As Equally Evil In All Communication.

Rome's choice of **how** to teach and critique what is sexual sin in *Catholic eyes* gives the non-verbal message that heterosexual intimacy, secondary to LLL being consummated outside the marital union (especially among the *vowed*), is as great a sin as the sexual intimacy in pedophilia, homosexuality and incest. (*Wow, I said it! This message has been an exceedingly aggravating irritant since, I can't remember when.*) After the human mind grasps the reality that *almost* one hundred percent of heterosexual couples (with friends I rarely shared I was a virgin when I married, because it was so uncomfortable to be such a gross minority) have sexual activity and sex before marriage, the additional non-verbal message that *grouping all sex sins under the same heading* gives a person is, "Hey, then sex with a child, daughter or the same sex, can't be that evil, either."

Why hasn't anyone openly questioned the non-verbal message the Catholic Church is giving, when they lump pedophilia, homosexuality, incest, etc., and the sex, which results from a man and woman falling *in love*, under the same heading, thus *degree* of sinfulness, thus laws? Have you found this so shocking, like me, there weren't even any words to express the confusion of, "How can this be?" Sex between a man and a woman in a heterosexual, *in love*, relationship, before/outside marriage, is as great a sin as the others? I don't think so! (How about, definitely not!?!) Yet, the perspective the Catholic Church perpetrates, with their choice of how to teach sexual issues, says just that. Even in the way the church has conducted its investigation to self-critique the compliance of *their own* ranks with church law, says just that.

In an official questionnaire given to the St. Paul and Minneapolis Diocesan priests in the late 1980's to assess the sexual status of their priests (and the potential likelihood of future law suits), the questions, which would indicate homosexual, pedophile or other ideophrenic tendencies, were randomly intermingled with questions, which could indicate a heterosexual, *in love*, LLL relationship. Talk about an Atomic Bomb of non-verbal communication! This questionnaire, alone, told all taking it that to be *in love* with a woman was as **sick** and sinful as ideophrenic sexual preferences. Believing this non-verbal message (similar to, if not, a subliminal message - we don't make a conscious choice whether to believe, or not) in ones **core being** makes it less difficult for the mind to transfer to ideophrenic sexual feelings, followed by said behavior. A great sadness, when those subliminal messages have been absorbed, is what circumstance or thought causes what *feeling(s)* changes, and unless we are sensitive enough to recognize the message, and negate it, our future choices, attitudes, what we suppress or repress, or see as *truth and/*or *good,* will be altered. When this *un-Godly lie* is accepted (voluntarily or involuntarily, and consciously or unconsciously) as truth, the person is much closer to the edge of the cliff, where, falling off would land him or her in a homosexual or worse, state of being. Because **"all sex, outside of a marriage, between a man and a woman,"** are grouped together as **ONE** issue, the latter (ideophrenic sexual desires and actions) are more likely to be *seen and felt* as ***normal.*** Add the ingredient, *when a person wants, and/or needs to see the church as infallible,* and it is that church delivering the message, there is almost a one hundred percent chance the non-verbal/subliminal message(s) will be absorbed as *truth* and *good*; no matter what is written as doctrine or verbally proclaimed.

I believe the paramount reason the Roman Catholic Church will not revise this deceptive (anti-God) way of visualizing the sins of sexuality is because this approach is its most powerful tool in brainwashing its vowed clergy, keeping its vowed from allowing any value to be attached to LLL feelings. The relevance of this piece of Catholic tradition slips by the minds of most Catholics; for they are not living a life style where it's affects are felt, so are unaware of its importance, but it landed right in my lap.

During the period of time Peter was genuinely researching what to give paramount value to in his life, after we had discovered each other, the Archdiocese of St Paul and Minneapolis had a sexuality workshop for its primary staff. The aforementioned questionnaire (Sexual Issues in Ministry [Response Day, February 9, 1988, March 3, 1988, April 7, 1988], Archdiocese of St. Paul and Minneapolis and Consultation Services Center) was the workshop's prime tool. Its affect on Peter was predictable. What normal adult male (or female) would want, could allow, himself/herself to FEEL IN THE SAME SINFUL STATE as those with ideophrenic sexual triggers? I couldn't! As serendipity (God's tool?) would have it, I came across this questionnaire when an unknown person had inadvertently, conveniently left it lying around as the workshop was in progress. After reading the information, and especially the questionnaire, I knew instantly where it would take Peter's mind (he wants to believe the church is omnipotent). I knew as one knows, but doesn't remember, they were in their mother's womb, that this presentation was anti-God, evil, *"power"* inspired, devil inspired, and calculated to achieve the hierarchies wanted result. But I had no credible way to communicate it to Peter or anyone else. After this workshop, Peter would just watch me with gaunt, devastatingly sad, hardened, desperate, and painful eyes (the same eyes were present after I sent him the roses, years and years later). If he ever does a *self-awareness search* to discover where and how non-verbal messages have affected him, I suspect he will find his *state of mind* was in a similar place after both, the workshop and the roses. What won? The non-verbal messages! This is a prime example of the power of non-verbal communication.

Another sad awareness? the extreme LONLINESS a priest lives out every day of his life <u>at the intimate level</u> (and especially on special holidays like Christmas and Easter, when the rest of the world is home with their families and intimate other), when combined with the aforesaid, pushes a celibate even closer to the edge of the aforementioned cliff.

V.) IF A PRIEST MARRIES HE IS EXCOMMUNICATED, PEDOPHILE PRIESTS WERE SENT TO OTHER PARISHES AND STILL, TODAY, ARE NOT EXCOMMUNICATED:

This action teaches the core of a person, especially the core of a person who believes the church is **omnipotent,** that marriage is a greater sin, when one has vowed to celibacy, than having sex with a child. This IS the non-verbal message, regardless of the massive amount of words the church hierarchy uses to neutralize the message or how doggedly they work to critique the messages from the liaisons stationed in every parish (at least in the St. Paul and Minneapolis Diocese), whose job it is to report any suspicious activity to the diocese.

Also, this is a **second** very powerful non-verbal, subliminal message, which says, "Loving a woman, of all things, is as repulsive and actually, more repulsive (when you want to be pleasing to the church and God), than ideophrenic sexual desires and actions! Despite their words, I think the church wants to have this message accepted!

VI.) CHANGING THE LANGUAGE, THUS MESSAGE, FOR THE SACRAMENT OF MARRIAGE (The other sacraments are acknowledged to be an outward sign of an inner state of being) **COMBINED WITH TEACHING THE PRESCENCE OF SOUL CONNECTING SEXUALITY IS FOR AFTER THE VOWS ARE MADE, ONLY** (What God has joined, let no man destroy), **COMBINED WITH SAYING NOTHING ABOUT WHAT SHOULD BE PRESENT BEFORE THE VOWS ARE SAID** gives the non-verbal message the vows allow, if not cause or insure that a sacramentally sealed union will have intimate, soul connecting sexual characteristics, especially if both partners are true to church laws. For most of my life, I wasn't even aware I had absorbed this message, but I had. I doubt I am an isolated case! At the thinking level it feels **ridiculous** to have absorbed it, but it's not the conscious process that critiques whether to accept or reject non-verbal messages, at least messages we have no education on how to identify. Find a quiet place and let your mind return to the days just before you decided to marry and during the betrothed period. Try to recall what thoughts and/or experiences caused what feelings and vise versa. If you believed you were *in love*, but had this, *"is this all there is?"* feeling following intimate sexual contact or told yourself practice would improve the experience and you still married, you may have absorbed this message without knowing it, too.

Combine this non-verbal message (VI) with number IV, and here lies a recipe leading to multiple numbers of God loving folks using the wrong information in trying to discern what God's will is for them, and how to identify who their life time mate is or isn't! This doesn't mean sexual freedom – God also wants celibacy outside the LLL union (the Bible verse about the *man who voluntarily restrains from sex for the Kingdom of God* does, even within the context of what society was at that time, supports this), which can use all the tools (and the church has them!) on how to maintain a celibate state the church can teach, to accomplish.

One thing about LLL, there will be no doubt what it is, when it arrives; so, when any doubt surfaces as to what your relationship is with another, it is NOT LLL.

To add to humanities confusion, someplace in history someone or some human institution(s) has been opportunistic and has erroneously expanded the meaning of the word, "LUST" to parallel the experience of the desires in the eroticism of LLL. This erroneous expansion of the meaning of the word *lust* has contributed to man's further invalidation of whole being erotic feelings for a woman and vise versa. With the lack of language to define the differences between pseudo-*in love* (friendship plus a satisfied *need or ego enhancement desire* combined with desires that originate from the physical) and LLL (where the physical symptoms are but a manifestation of what has happened to and is present in the soul and mind), manipulating the meaning of "*lust,*" to place the feeling of guilt on any sexual pleasure wasn't all that difficult.

Webster's New World Dictionary

"Lust 1. bodily appetite; esp., excessive sexual desire. 2. over mastering a desire; as in lust for power. *v.i.* to feel an intense desire, especially sexual desire."

Catholic Reference Encyclopedia

"Lust An inordinate appetite for sexual gratification. It is one of the seven capital sins and leads to such other grave sins as adultery, fornication, incest and sodomy. God has attached pleasure to the sexual act to induce man to propagate the race. This pleasure is forbidden to all unmarried persons. The tendency in man's nature to seek inordinate sexual gratification proceeds from concupiscence, which is a result of original sin."

Hmmm! Think I've just discovered a major contributor to who erroneously expanded the meaning of the word *lust*. It is no wonder mankind is confused. LLL is very exclusive; it is not sex just to have sex. LLL desires ONENESS with the other and sex is a fraction of this whole process. From the definition in the Catholic Reference Encyclopedia, it's very apparent the core issue is, **we need to find language to communicate LLL**, for now there is none. It is no wonder innocent people have defined their experiences erroneously. The *Powers* have eradicated LLL's existence from human awareness by eradicating or refusing to develop language to communicate it. Let us pray.

Psalm 60:12 "With God's help we shall do mighty things, for he will trample down our foes."[37]

---

[37] A translation from The Book (a version of The Living Bible) Tyndale House Publishers.

The vow of marriage needs to be proclaimed as an outward sign of an already existing *state of being* in a heterosexual relationship, just as the other sacraments are proclaimed to be an outward sign of an inner state of being. Why did the church change its language for the Sacrament of Marriage? This was no accident; it was an intricately thought out manipulation of words.

VII.) JUST THAT A PRIEST CAN TAKE THE VOW OF CHASTITY

gives the message the priest taking the vow believes the Roman Catholic Church's non-verbal messages, has absorbed (voluntarily or involuntarily, and consciously or unconsciously) the subliminal messages that celibacy is more pleasing to God than a heterosexual intimate lifetime union with **NO exceptions** (regardless of what their lips say). When celibates are in each other's company, no heterosexual sexually active folks present, a manifestation of this absorption is the joy felt when mocking anything in a heterosexual relationship's life style (a characteristic of homosexuals, also, but their mocking is usually a more direct attack on the female in the heterosexual relationship).

When a priest finds himself without energy to seriously consider the viewpoints of a woman (no time to listen) or his reflex response is to NOT believe the words coming out of the mouth of a woman or worse, he has probably absorbed the church's non-verbal message, "God does not want females to represent Him on earth" message, too. (As a matter of fact, if you find yourself mocking or devaluing the words on these pages, it is quite possible you have absorbed, even unwittingly, this non-verbal message, for the messages in this book are through the mind of a female.) If a man had not absorbed either or both of these messages he couldn't allow himself to make the Vow of Chastity in the first place.

The only exceptions to these generalizations I can think of is, when a man's motivation for joining the priesthood is homosexually motivated (he wouldn't be tempted to marry, anyway), or his LLL other died, or is obviously out of reach.

Those who believe God about the *goodness* of *marriage should be very concerned and verbal about these non-verbal, subliminal, messages,* if for no other reason, married folks are not secondhand citizens in God's eye. And even if you didn't absorb these non-verbal messages, *your child may.*

VIII.) THEIR WORDS SAY, REMAINING IN THE PRIESTHOOD IS VOLUNTARY. THE TRAINING GIVEN PRIESTS LEAVES THEM NO OTHER OPTION BUT TO REMAIN.

Is anything for self-preservation really voluntary? Because the church has arranged consequences of such severe magnitude for those finding the celibate priesthood is not for them, the church is making it mandatory to stay, is making their system a prison with walls as high as infinity. The church not only refuses dispensations, their seminaries close doors on training that could transfer to any other career of comparable status. What does a priest, who has left its ranks, do in the community to keep food on the table, a roof over his head, and his self worth intact? The church's answer? Nothing! They decline to support any other career, even in the church, another most UN-GOD LIKE treatment of Godly men. Obviously the church wants this individual to perceive the pains of survival, because of their withheld training, in the general society as punishment from God for not keeping their vow, and tragically, this is the end result for too many who have left. (So, cheer up! Stop feeling guilty. The difficulties you are experiencing in society, outside the active priesthood, ARE NOT FROM GOD! They are the product of master manipulators, earth bound master manipulators who saw to it you would feel this way.) The non-verbal message, the prison walls to infinity for those finding they have made a mistake – is – it is more Godly to anesthetize yourself with alcohol, mood elevators and antidepressants than it is to leave the priesthood. The church refuses to see the pain is from the *"self" being destroyed.* (The *"self,"* as in Matthew 16:26.)

The advice my brother received, which literally saved his life, is the exact opposite. If my brother was to maintain sobriety and survive, he had to abandon the family farm and find his tools for survival in society elsewhere. True, he didn't spend eight plus years in college and thousands of dollars for an education or told he was going to Hell for breaking a vow, but a common denominator with many priests is, he had accepted what his life career would be (for my brother it was the farm) without question, no other avenue felt open to him, but he found a pain there so great he had to anesthetize himself. This place is where many a priest has found himself. Are you a priest on medication to alter your mental status (example: Prozac, Celexa or Wellbutrin) or still drinking? If you want to save your *'"self," from destruction,* as in **Matthew 16:26** (The New American Bible translation),

"(26) What profit would a man show if he were to gain the whole world and destroy himself in the process? **What can a man offer in exchange for his very self?"**

you had better race to the nearest AA meeting, toss the pills and alcohol enroute and probably resign your priestly position. At least there is hope you will be able to keep your *"self"* alive outside the walls of the Catholic priesthood, without analgesics and mood elevators. The *"self"* is your only direct communication with God!

If we are to be wise, intelligent, Godly people, we need to develop tools to identify, and then, negate anti-God non-verbal messages. One huge test to be given any situation in life is: "If the *words* are not ONE with the *non-verbal message(s),* the WHOLE situation is NOT God's, our Lord and Savior through Jesus Christ's, doing." God had nothing to do with what the perpetrators are trying to achieve. More and more people are reaching this higher level of consciousness where they are seeing and confronting anti-God non-verbal messages; i.e., confronting those who give anti-truth non-verbal messages (the message expressed in words would be NOT accepted), or one message with their lips and a conflicting message with their behavior, choices and mandates. One such person with a higher level of consciousness is the reporter who reported the firing of the diocesan editor.

God answers idolatry; He nullifies His power over evil in those bowing before idols, which allows depression (anger at self for going against God, for at a deep level they know they did), varying degrees of *multiple personality disorder* (the personality breaks into pieces to survive pain, each piece trying to accomplish conflicting goals or conflicting means to reach a said goal) and *sexual deviations* are formed as a result of the previous generation(s) going against God's intimacy plans, which were perpetrated by idolaters. How many alcoholic priests are there who are now being medicated with mood elevators? The hierarchy's recipe for crushing LLL unions works. Their recipe works so well, those who want *their will to be done, not God's,* have followed it down to *the* minutest detail for *so many centuries,* many believe it is a *Godly* deed to crush LLL, when it interferes with mankind's desires. Mankind is now *in the blind* and can't even fathom the wonderful plan God had for His people. Our own brain and soul cause the wanted physical responses in a healthy body, when LLL is the adhesive in a couple's relationship; no drugs are needed (Cialas, Levitra or Viagra). Then, add to the above, <u>Hurt People Hurt People.</u>[38] This piece, also, is so

---

[38] Hurt People Hurt People is written by Sandra Wilson.

huge, books and books have not covered all the damage. When individuals are so consumed with their believed, albeit anti-God ideal, that they accept depression (taking anti-depressants has become an accepted norm!), accept having a different personality for every occasion (what one sees as valuable depends on which personality is in charge at the moment; and the vacillating desires makes it even harder to distinguish what is *from God)*, sexual deviations (striving for legal homosexual marriages says they believe they are normal), and mortally wounding (destroys hope and/or trust) the one they *do love with their whole being,* rather than confront the system, the Roman Catholic Church (or other oppressive entity), what other choice does God have but to damage the system, Himself? Almost all the perspectives of western world culture are derived from the Roman Catholic Church for almost all Christian churches commenced in Catholicism, Catholicism or Eastern Orthodox (both have roots in Judaism). "There are no accidents," the work of God's hand is blatantly visible; Boston just closed seventy parishes in one clean sweep! (May 2004) and the Portland Diocese (July 2004) has filed for bankruptcy. (How many more will follow? And for the rest of the world it is just the beginning. As reported in the Minneapolis Star Tribune, the Archdiocese of Vienna Austria substantiates a report that forty thousand pornographic pictures, including child porn, were in the *accessible to all* computer system of a Catholic seminary fifty miles west of Vienna.) Each of us is a Temple of God and God is working through each of us to correct The Temple.

"Oh," you say, "but the church does so much *good*!" and I agree. Albeit, everything in this world is *good AND bad.* When the *bad* tips the scale, God's people have a responsibility to acknowledge *it* openly, to make decisions on who to actively support accordingly, to correct *it*, or, we and our children sink with *it*. (Even a convict guilty of numerous murders can do loving things for his mother or his wife and family, but this doesn't negate the sin of *murder,* or make it acceptable to continue murdering innocent people. Various *"mafias"* of the world survive and their members attend church, because their minds are warped on this issue.) The Roman Catholic

Church has NOT corrected the *bad*; they have actually reinforced the *bad* (their return to an increased legalistic life approach in negating Vatican II is a return to the lifestyle that conceived, nurtured and perpetrated the ideophrenic sexuality in the first place!) to camouflage the *evil* more. Man! those in Rome must have loved their power in days past; they are working so hard against God to regain it. Some United State's Cardinals mourn the decrease in their power so much they are attempting to reinstate their Medieval power by refusing those in the public eye communion if they are affiliated with an organization supporting free choice, birth control or stem cell research. (This is also good diversion from betrayal of children sins.) What is the non-verbal message here? Ones personal conscience has no value; church law will get you to Heaven. Denying *truth* **IS** denying God, and we answer to God for following *our conscience,* not for following Roman Catholic Church law. Not being truthful in verbal and non-verbal messages is making yourself God. Nothing from this earth will invalidate what life experience teaches, for, whatever the pain in our life experience, finding the true **root** of the pain, and repairing it is the grand design of God to bring us closer to where God wants us to be. Keep asking questions!

I was in the belief Rome needed to do ONE thing to show they *see* their contributions to and take responsibility for the massive number of cases of child abuse/betrayal – rescind their celibacy mandates for the priesthood and other vocations. Because of recent developments, I need to add a second condition the public may need in order to be able to trust Rome again. The second condition is that they deny themselves the Holy Eucharist for an extended period of time as penance for their betrayal of the children sins. What is good for the goose is good for the gander, right? All leaders, to be God pleasing leaders, need to live by the same rules they impose on their subordinates.

Even though climbing the mountain road from accepting and believing forced celibacy, the vow of Chastity, for the priesthood is most pleasing to God, - to- LLL is God's dominant plan/most gracious plan for His people, would rival <u>The Road of Blood,</u> the name given to the road from

Jericho (1,300 feet below sea level) to Jerusalem (2,600 feet above sea level), the church needs to commence the trip. With God's help, they can do it, and bring many, many people home to where their hearts are, the Roman Catholic Church. The sobering fact that for the first time in US history, the people are turning out in greater numbers for protestant services than for Catholic services accentuates a major shift in the beliefs of the Catholic mass consciousness. It reminds me of an attempted, but failed suicide; all these Catholics, who have left the Roman Catholic Church and are being active in other Christian churches, are crying, "Help! Please Rome, Help! Help us to be able to *trust* you again!"

    The Canon Law side of the Roman Catholic Church could ENDEAR itself to the Theological side, instead of minimizing the Theological side into nothingness as they did, when they eradicated any money to support Catholic schools and universities if their teachings contradicted Canon Law. The Theology side of the church is the church I love so dearly. It gives credibility to an individual's mind and acknowledges, there are *gray areas* where we don't have the answers and, "Yes, this is possible!" or, "Yes, that is possible," is an acceptable response. At least this was true before Rome withheld their monetary support. When the Canon Law side of the church can respect the Theology side, substantially, maybe, just maybe the Roman Catholic Church can successfully ascend <u>The Road of Blood</u>. Can the *Canon Law* side and the *Theology* side be ONE? It cannot be said too often, Jesus consistently emphasized the framework of **ONE**, *one* with God, *one* with each other in marriage, the Trinity (God, the Holy Spirit and Jesus) is *One*. Surely Rome would find God's Light in unifying the Canon Law side and Theology side by allowing Theology more freedom to influence church law. (Now that would be a marriage I'd like to witness!) A healthy start would be to relinquish the requirements now applied to the distribution of Vatican funds, as mentioned above.

    So, if anyone reading this have credentials, doctorate(s) in Theology and/or Psychology, and finds what I've shared goes right to your heart, **your** *life-experience* has taught you some if not all of the truths mentioned, and you feel the truth in the messages in this book; please don't hesitate to step forward with your support. This world requires *credentials* to accomplish almost anything, and since the leaders of the church have spent their whole lives *in study*, they likely do not respect information from anyone with fewer credits to their name than they possess; and that's even questionable. God's people need those with documented intellectual power to affect Rome, so they will correct their non-verbal messages, re-prioritize their view of God's preferences, and change their laws accordingly. It may be too late for us, but it is NOT too late for our children and grandchildren.

I pray for your help.

X
GOD IS THE LIGHT
WHEN DAY TURNS TO NIGHT

Peter did reluctantly admit to me that he has been told he suffers from depression. Apparently various psychological tests brought this knowledge forward. (He's the opposite of depressed when I'm around.) In God's Word to me He has frequently validated that Peter is depressed ("exiled to Egypt," the words in the Bible on the *plane of the individual*). As the years roll by and I trust more of the deductions my mind makes about what I see, I am becoming more convinced he has some mild *multiple personality*-like issues, also. Many times, even though our visits have been infrequent, he has complained he is always vacillating on what he wants to do, one tangible symptom. What he wants to do probably depends on which personality is in charge of him at a particular time. I pray the **Peter** God made is the **Peter** who survives.

Yes, all this can be classified as *normal* (we have come to accept this way of living even though it is the opposite of ONE). It is quite evident that, to the best of his ability, Peter is trying to manifest what he perceives as right and good, and God must be pleased with him for working so hard to live according to his, even though *brain washed* (these words do describe what anti-God, non-verbal communication accomplishes), conscience. In my moments of weakness and woundedness, I do wonder if God is so pleased with Peter's intentions He has abandoned His will for *"us-together."* The path of least resistance would be to let the pain from rejection take me over, and I could/would sink out of life, but God isn't letting me off the hook this easy. He is demanding I rejoice in His glory and all the glorious things He has done for me and write what He has shown me down on paper, this book. (I have a new, strong empathy for Jonah.)

Since Peter chooses *death* (he chose to kill *who* and *how* God made him, which blocks the manifestation of God's will for him/in him), rather than jeopardize his role as a priest, there are no possibilities to follow *God's will* to him or vise versa. Over the years I have attempted to communicate with him about some of the pieces I have shared on these pages, but his response was parallel to how the Jewish leaders responded when they were caught in their dilemma about whether John the Baptist was a messenger from God, or not. They answered, "We don't know." (Mark 11:30-33) Peter's words were either he hadn't had an opportunity to read whatever piece I gave him, or he claimed he didn't understand what I was saying. The dilemma in his mind, most likely, was that he wanted to be compliant with what his leaders taught him to do with me, but he also wanted to avoid any conflict which would make me leave and never return again. It is also possible he really couldn't disgrace me directly by telling me that since those thoughts came out of the mind of a woman (words to this extent have actually made him angry), but the *feelings* he likely has, which resulted from the non-verbal language being absorbed, surely could cause the end result, <u>no energy to clarify his thoughts and beliefs for a woman</u>. Anytime a female makes a challenging remark the mind would say, "Why take time away from something worthwhile to clarify for her?" In other words, if the mental images, which derogate any information from a woman, could talk they would say something to the affect, "Neither Jesus nor the church want females to represent him (Jesus) on this earth, how can I give thoughts from a female any valuable time or validity in my mind when they didn't, and don't?" If he didn't understand and wanted to, he would have asked questions, but none were asked; he did not want to understand. His choice, death, is the "worm that ate through the stem of the plant (any hope for a future with us in each other's lives) so that it (any hope for loves constancy) withered and died." (Jonah 4:7) The last of the rare self-disclosures he made was that he wondered if there really was life after death (from the mouth of a priest?); either he's *been told something I haven't,* he was mocking my perceived naiveté, or a lot has withered and died.

Where does LLL go when hope is dead? To God and God does keep reinforcing He will have Peter and I together one day. But what feels more plausible, painfully plausible, especially if Peter ever reads these pages, is instead, he will transfer his love to hate. It feels as though he already has and is manifesting his hate by deciding LLL is so painful, it needs to be avoided at all cost. All cost? Here this means he will even decide the celibate life style is the only hope of avoiding LLL, thus the pain it has caused in him. I'm almost positive the words flowing across his mind about his relationship with me are, "If only I had followed the (*prescribed by orthodox)* teachers and counselors support for the celibate life style protocol to a "T", I wouldn't be in so much pain." If we were communicating, I would definitely need to confront him about such a deduction, for I can see he is erroneously accusing LLL. LLL rained joy and happiness on Peter; it was the prevention of contact with each other that caused the pain, not LLL. The LLL did happen as he was living the *"protocol for the celibate life style;"* even if he had not slipped (God actually pushed him!) and consummated our relationship, the LLL would still be. So the only element, which could be changed that would have prevented the pain, is if we could have been allowed to be together within the framework, and with the blessings of that which defines his being, the Roman Catholic Priesthood, which God also called him to. If Peter could erase the ramifications of the non-verbal language of the church at his core, and/or been allowed *time* to think at all (because of the shortage of priests they are kept so busy they hardly have time to eat or sleep; but then, being they're always involved in social events, maybe they are actually avoiding *feeling* and thinking time), he may have seen, "which came first, the chicken or the egg?" At least, I pray so. The evidence which tells me Peter is accusing the wrong entity (LLL) for his pain is his missing name on the list of names of the St. Paul and Minneapolis Diocese area priests, who signed the letter to the Bishops requesting mandatory celibacy for parish priests be discussed; the now infamous letter of the 113. (December 2003)

Hate victimizes its owner so I am putting all the energy I have toward avoiding the insidious condition. Putting the energy out to organize my aware nesses and writing this book is my transfer of energy; "The truth will set you free." And so it is. I can say Peter continues to evoke LLL feelings in me, but whether I could ever allow myself to be vulnerable to the pain of his rejections again, I don't know. Yes, God does say I must forgive as He has forgiven us, but I still don't know. I don't know if I have the inner energy left to live with *"not being worthy of truth"* at the intimate level (the outgrowth of the centuries lived in the shadow of Non-verbal Message number II). Between the truth the physician and my ex-husband withheld from me about my own being (the source of the sexually transmitted disease), and the truth Peter withheld from me, I don't know if I could ever trust a man was allowing me the *whole truth* or just allowing me what he wanted me to hear to protect his needs and interests. "Trust" is a delicate place; Peter did make me into nothing more than road kill time after time. God picked me up, sent me looking for answers, and showed me answers. As a *zebra cannot change its stripes*, I have accepted that Peter cannot change what he has been internalizing since he was a young lad, the non-verbal messages of that which he loves, the Roman Catholic Church; it is now *who* he is, his *"self"* is being destroyed (is he on mood elevators or frequently drinking alcohol?) or has been destroyed. The fact he *could* vow to celibacy attests to the degree of his absorption. It feels eerily ironic that the last homily I heard him give was about the power of non-verbal communication! Needless to say, he did not give any examples, which involved the church. (Another serendipitous event: I was working on the non-verbal communication piece of this book when I heard this homily.) I do believe he won't ask my forgiveness or understanding with the intention of or hope that we could be more involved in each others life experience so I don't believe I'll have the opportunity to discover whether I can forgive at my deepest level - in *real* life. When I consider that absorbing non-verbal messages is, most often, involuntary, there is hope; but my mind can still see too clearly, the vigorousness with which he wiped his cheek after I had bestowed a *butterfly kiss* upon it. I know he feared some lipstick remained there, but the energy he emanated to be secure there was no trace remaining rivaled how one would scrub to remove poison ivy (a powerful non-verbal message). He regrets the one church law he broke, has obeyed every one of the others, and does not want any doubt in anyone's mind, about his faithfulness to the vows he made to his church, or, his faithfulness to his church. "With God all things are possible," but even for God, winning over a *free will* so engrained with anti-intimate-heterosexual-relationship beliefs, especially since these beliefs are reinforced and reinforced and reinforced in their retreats and counseling centers for their clerics, will be near impossible.

What I would do, if I could do, is ascend to the plane above our physical body and have my soul apologize to his soul. His consciousness wouldn't understand (the muddy water has blinded him), but his soul would. I would apologize for not taking more risks to show him what *God's wants* are before he had descended to the depths of the unreachable. And probably the greatest of all my sins are I didn't follow God when he told me not to marry my high school sweetheart. (God's message finally made it through to my conscious mind during our marriage ceremony! And at that time in my life, I couldn't believe those messages in my head were *God inspired.)* Maybe, just maybe God would have had Peter and I meet before he said his vows. More recently, I know I should have aggressively confronted him when I felt the angels fighting for him to *see* and *hear*, after my (non) confession. A simple passionate kiss from the soul may have catapulted his consciousness into *hearing the angels*, too. But he may have also diminished my value in his eyes to a demonic power, as documented history says has happened. God's Word supports the *"hearing the angels"* outcome.

"I apologize, oh soul of Peter. I am sorry I was not *stronger-in-the-Lord*." Like *No-Fault* car insurance emphasizes, some responsibility falls on both parties.

The conscious process that has deduced the thoughts on these pages has a closing awareness to share. On the *plane of the world*, an undeniable common denominator throughout recorded history is "man killing man in the name of God". It's a breath taking realization, *gasping for air* realization, that *today* the war on terrorism is a war of Christian/Jew versus Muslim, a "man killing man in the name of God" war, which has continued for over two thousand plus, plus, plus, years. It is a war, which is still threatening the safety of God's people! On the *plane of the individual*, another perspective the world's history and present day turmoil can be surmised as is; "throughout history, when God has showered LLL on the earth, the earth has greeted God's gift/blessing/mandate with blood shed; those of the world would rather kill than risk denting any accumulated wealth and power. Until the human race can *accept* that every individual is precious in God's eyes, that a man and a woman crossing boundaries (*power* boundaries, *monetary* boundaries, *religious, race, nationality,* you name it!), to unite, is pleasing to God, and that the earth's social entities will maintain their wealth and power if they follow God in every aspect, from the *plane of the individual* through the *plane of the community* to *the plane of the world*, and revise their laws to support the LLL/HOLY/Sacramental (as the Theology side of the church has defined it) unions, only then will mankind *see* an end to war. Even going to war to control oil fields or any of earth's riches, pales in the light of what the world has done to control which man joins with which woman, which does determined who retains the control of the wealth and power in the world; who will control and enjoy your accumulated riches when you die?

Life Light Love is like the "Rose trampled on the ground..."

Everyday now, there is *something* which validates the paramount importance of God's LLL, **Life Light Love**, condition. When we have freed our minds from the cesspool of sin, the idol worship, which causes depression, denial, lies, multiple personalities to survive this world, and dependence on pain killers and mood elevators, we are free to see and live in the beauty of Agape and Eros (the *pure* Eros, which needs God's Word to describe it, LLL, not an emotional misinterpretation). Sooner or later, in those who *want* and *work* for *good*, LLL will be tangibly manifested in each of us to a most undeniable degree. Since this perspective has consciously taken root, I cannot believe how valuable I see every life, *every life*. Inevitably, all will be punished who deny and/or denounce it, repress and/or suppress it.

There is HOPE, hope the true intentions behind demeaning LLL and women are being recognized by the literate and educated masses. Just last week, I heard another book has been published contending the same deductions; protecting the powers, which control *who* marries *who* (thus off-spring, thus the wealth of the world), is a core reason for the wars in this world. How ironic, sad and tragic this is also a paramount reason God's Temples have been polluted. And, if mankind ceased to control marriage? gradually, the reasons for protecting ones accumulated wealth and territory or gaining territory would lose value, become a non-issue. I heard this proclamation upon turning the radio on during my afternoon commute. I missed the name of the book; I missed the name of the author. It appears my research has not ended!

I am definitely not a scholar; I am definitely not a writer. But, when the present books being written about romantic love, or trouble with romantic relationships reference another author to give their work credibility, chances are I have read 95-100% of the works being referenced. This realization allows me the courage to present the perspective found on these pages. I concur with the metaphor, "If God could be seen as a combination of the sun and ocean, and humanity is the reflective sparkles from the sun off the ocean's surface, I am but one sparkle." I am not a Theologian; I am not a Canon Lawyer. But I love the reverence for God, the praise, glory and worship of the Trinity found in Catholicism. Conversely, I see the pain this earth born institution has rained on humanity throughout the ages. Why? What happened to God's plan? Your brain is *good*, God made it. (Yes, this is contrary to what various religions promote; "man is inherently evil," therefore we cannot trust our own minds. Watching a baby and young toddler with educated and sensitive eyes will erase this belief from your mind.) I pray to God you *try this shoe* (trusting your own mind while reading these pages) *on for size* in the recollections of your life. It is very basic what brought me to these truths; it is the *thinking* my father called *common sense*, the same thinking which describes a pair of warm boots for this Minnesota winter. "I like those boots," he'd say, "they're practical!" Combine the *common sense* with double, no, quadruple doses of *prayer* and you have the recipe.

My oldest daughter passed the following onto me. It sums-up what we truly need to do with the *brains* our glorious God gave us.

"Not to know is bad. Not to want to know is worse." -West African proverb

What happens when you don't know the answer to a question? Do you forget about it, or find out about it? You may have heard the saying "Ignorance is bliss." Don't believe it. Instead, ask questions. Be curious. Have an inquiring mind -- and never give up. If you really want to know something, keep searching for the answer. If other people don't know it and you can't find it in books, you may have to discover it for yourself.

Today: I'll be a curious cat." [39]

Not following this wisdom has dire ramifications. My mother's rage, which owned her unto death, was because life didn't turn out the way she felt she had been promised if she intricately followed the teachings and laws of the Roman Catholic Church. She felt as though she was sinning if she asked questions. She felt betrayed, but couldn't own where the betrayal originated. So **ask questions!** before the momentum of your life and the passing of time closes and *dead bolts* all the doors and you are **locked in** where you are.

And my added thought? TRUST **God-in-you**. TRUST what your God given brain *sees* and *follow* His lead in your life's path. God will lead the way.

Before the last words of this book are written, our Lord God has a message for all reading these pages: "If you are one, who in the past, believed in Love, *in-love,* and the momentum of today's earth message (it has no value) has stolen HOPE from your heart, rise up and rejoice! For again I say, when the good man turns to evil, he shall die[40] (the *self* that hears God is no more). Rise up and rejoice, for as the words on these pages indicate, I am alive and will return. And I will bring with me all that I have promised."

The following is a wonderful example of God's work when our *free will,* on *the plane of the community* and the *individual,* allows it, and how God does overcome the forces of evil on earth.

---

[39] Espeland P. Wallner, R. Making the Most of Today. (1991). Minneapolis, MN.
[40] Ezekiel 33:18, As translated in The Book.

THE TABLECLOTH

The brand new pastor and his wife, newly assigned to their first ministry, to reopen a church in suburban Brooklyn, arrived in early October excited about their opportunities. When they saw their church, it was very run down and needed much work. They set a goal to have everything done in time to have their first service on Christmas Eve.

They worked hard, repairing pews, plastering walls, painting, etc. and on Dec 18 were ahead of schedule and just about finished. On Dec 19 a terrible tempest - a driving rainstorm - hit the area and lasted for two days. On the 21st, the pastor went over to the church. His heart sank when he saw that the roof had leaked, causing a large area of plaster about 20 feet by 8 feet to fall off the front wall of the sanctuary just behind the pulpit, beginning about head high.

The pastor cleaned up the mess on the floor, and not knowing what else to do but postpone the Christmas Eve service, headed home. On the way he noticed that a local business was having a flea market type sale for charity so he stopped in. One of the items was a beautiful, handmade, ivory colored, crocheted tablecloth with exquisite work, fine colors and a Cross embroidered right in the center. It was just the right size to cover up the hole in the front wall. He bought it and headed back to the church.

By this time it had started to snow. An older woman running from the opposite direction was trying to catch the bus. She missed it. The pastor invited her to wait in the warm church for the next bus 45 minutes later. She sat in a pew and paid no attention to the pastor while he got a ladder, hangers, etc., to put up the tablecloth as a wall tapestry.

The pastor could hardly believe how beautiful it looked and it covered up the entire problem area. Then he noticed the woman walking down the center aisle. Her face was like a sheet. "Pastor," she asked, "where did you get that tablecloth?"

THE FLYING SCROLL

The pastor explained. The woman asked him to check the lower right corner to see if the initials, EBG were crocheted into it there. They were. These were the initials of the woman, and she had made this tablecloth 35 years before, in Austria. The woman could hardly believe it as the pastor told how he had just gotten the tablecloth.

The woman explained that before the war she and her husband were well-to-do people in Austria. When the Nazis came, she was forced to leave. Her husband was going to follow her the next week. She was captured, sent to prison and never saw her husband or her home again. The pastor wanted to give her the tablecloth; but she made the pastor keep it for the church.

The pastor insisted on driving her home, that was the least he could do. She lived on the other side of Staten Island and was only in Brooklyn for the day for a housecleaning job.

What a wonderful service they had on Christmas Eve. The church was almost full. The music and the spirit were great. At the end of the service, the pastor and his wife greeted everyone at the door and many said that they would return. One older man, whom the pastor recognized from the neighborhood, continued to sit in one of the pews and stare, and the pastor wondered why he wasn't leaving. The man asked him where he got the tablecloth on the front wall because it was identical to one that his wife had made years ago when they lived in Austria before the war and how could there be two tablecloths so much alike?

He told the pastor how the Nazis came, how he forced his wife to flee for her safety, and he was supposed to follow her, but he was arrested and put in a prison. He never saw his wife or his home again all the 35 years in between. The pastor asked him if he would allow him to take him for a little ride. They drove to Staten Island and to the same house where the pastor had taken the woman three days earlier. He helped the man climb the three flights of stairs to the woman's apartment, knocked on the door and he saw the greatest Christmas reunion he could ever imagine.

True Story - submitted by Pastor Rob Reid -- Who says God does work in mysterious ways?

> I asked the Lord to bless you as
> I prayed for you today.
> To guide you and protect you as
> you go along your way...
> .His love is always with you,
> His promises are true,
> And when we give Him all our cares you know
> He will see us through.
> So when the road you're traveling on seems difficult at best,
> Just remember I'm here praying, and God will do the rest. "[41]

"GOD REIGNS"   AMEN

---

[41] (Received via Email) Subject: Fw: [Fwd: The Tablecloth], Date: Wed, 20 Aug 2003 23:06:02 -0500

Epilogue

God's timing is perfect. Mankind needed until *now* to learn and live God's ways before we could absorb the larger picture of His truth. Like Jesus' words in **Mark 2:22,**

> " (22)You know better than to put new wine into old wineskins. They will burst. The wine would be spilled out and the wineskins ruined. New wine needs fresh wineskins."[42]

We would have *burst* if we would have heard (new to us) God's corrections before we were ready to hear them. For only in living what we *believe* are God's instructions can we see our mistakes, can we believe, be convinced, that we had misunderstood some of His very important, essential, instructions. All too often, the "*self*" can deny what the "*self*" sees until it is too late to alter our path, and for some, they deny unto death.

I pray The Flying Scroll aids you and yours in finding the strength needed to defeat DENIAL, while there is still time for you and yours to change life's path, if you need to, and thus have time to discover and to revel in *God's glorious plan for His people* before your physical death. Amen.

---

[42] Translation from The Book (a version of the Living Bible), Tyndale House Publishers.

Post Script:

Dear Reader, Child of God,

Now, having organized my awarenesses and transcribed them into writing, I can truly say my body, mind and Spirit are ONE.

May God's beautiful and intense Light and Love be over, under, around and through you, now and forever.

"Through Jesus Christ, with Him and in Him, in the unity of the Holy Spirit, all glory and honor is yours Almighty Father, forever and ever. Amen"

With most sincerity,
Pat Hockel

I know there is something I need to learn

from you,

so please contact me.

plhockel@email.com

or

Pat Hockel
P.O. Box 704
Prior Lake, MN 55372

> How To Obtain A Copy Of The Flying Scroll:
>
> May be ordered from any Barnes and Nobles Book Store. Internet:
> Amazon.com
> AuthorHouse.com
> BarnesandNoble.com
> www.TheFlyingScroll.com

About The Author

What is most important for you to know is what the author believes, and I quote:

"The thesis of this book, 'trust yourself, God-in-you,' is the message that is necessary to actualize God's will for you and who God puts in your path. The truth in any situation I describe that can be transferred to experiences in your life must *connect the dots* of what your ears have heard and your eyes have seen, also. If the proposed 'truth(s)' do not – that alone invalidates this information; ten doctorates would not alter that end result."

Ms. Hockel has had half a century of life experience, is employed as a Registered Nurse, has two adult daughters and two grandchildren. She learned the cause and effect of life's forces early in life, secondary to the birth of a congenitally deformed sister and a verbally abusive mother, all while observing and maturing within the practicalities of living on a farm. In her adult life she has constantly had communication with the human race during sickness and crisis when all but God, love, and caring have lost value.

A smile crosses her face as she recalls the wisdom her father shared with her in her youth during those long hours walking the bean fields (to excise the sprouted corn from the previous year's crop) beside him. "Think about that, Pat," he'd say; "Think about that," was his frequent response to any of her apparent immature inquiries about life or shared erroneous perspectives. She has survived *life* (which includes the death of her sister and both parents and divorce) because she believes God is actively leading *the way*, and as you will discover, she has "thought about that," a lot.